Who Is a Christian?

Zacchaeus Studies: New Testament

General Editor: Mary Ann Getty, RSM

Who Is a Christian?
A Study in Pauline Ethics

by

Robert F. O'Toole, S.J.

A Michael Glazier Book
THE LITURGICAL PRESS
Collegeville, Minnesota

A Michael Glazier Book
published by
THE LITURGICAL PRESS

Typography by Brenda Belizzone and Cyndi Cohee.

1   2   3   4   5   6   7   8   9

Library of Congress Cataloging-in-Publication Data

O'Toole, Robert F.
    Who is a Christian? : a study in Pauline ethics / by Robert F. O'Toole.
        p.   cm. — (Zacchaeus studies. New Testament)
    "A Michael Glazier book."
    Includes bibliographical references and index.
    ISBN 0-8146-5678-1
    1. Christian ethics—Biblical teaching. 2. Bible. N.T. Epistles
of Paul—Criticism, interpretation, etc. I. Title. II. Series.
BS2655.E8O76   1990
241'.092'4—dc19
                                  89-30010
                                  CIP

To my grandmother,
Margaret Mary Kenny Earner,
who believed and lived Paul's message.

Contents

Editor's Note

Zacchaeus Studies provide concise, readable and relatively inexpensive scholarly studies on particular aspects of scripture and theology. The New Testament section of the series presents studies dealing with focal or debated questions; and the volumes focus on specific texts of particular themes of current interest in biblical interpretation. Specialists have their professional journals and other forums where they discuss matters of mutual concern, exchange ideas and further contemporary trends of research; and some of their work on contemporary biblical research is now made accessible for students and others in *Zacchaeus Studies*.

The authors in this series share their own scholarship in non-technical language, in the areas of their expertise and interest. These writers stand with the best in current biblical scholarship in the English-speaking world. Since most of them are teachers, they are accustomed to presenting difficult material in comprehensible form without compromising a high level of critical judgment and analysis.

The works of this series are ecumenical in content and purpose and cross credal boundaries. They are designed to augment formal and informal biblical study and discussion. Hopefully they will also serve as texts to enhance and supplement seminary, university and college classes. The series will also aid Bible study groups, adult education and parish religious education classes to develop intelligent, versatile and challenging programs for those they serve.

Mary Ann Getty
New Testament Editor

Introduction

Paul's genuine epistles (1 Thess, 1 & 2 Cor, Gal, Rom, Phil, and Phlm) constitute the basis for the present discussion. These are the letters which the vast majority of scholars attribute to Paul. Consequently, this presentation limits itself to them and strives to bring the reader into direct contact with what Paul himself writes.

Paul, in his letters, does not present either a complete systematic theology nor an exhaustive morality. Of course, "morality" frequently looks to the actual conduct of men and women, while "ethics" determines the principles and judgments which lead to such conduct.[1] But since many authors do not distinguish between these two terms, neither will I. Our interest is, however, in what Paul has to say on either of these levels. These data in Paul can be isolated and summarized. In fact, the scope of this book is to consider mostly those passages

---

[1]E.g. Robert J. Daly *et al, Christian Biblical Ethics: From Biblical Revelation to Contemporary Christian Praxis, Method and Content* (New York: Paulist, 1984) 92f; William C. Spohn, *What Are They Saying about Scripture and Ethics* (New York: Paulist, 1984) 3. Here, too, the point raised by S. Schulz ("Der frühe und der späte Paulus: Uberlegungen zur Entwicklung seiner Theologie und Ethik," *TZ* 41 [1985] 228-36), who contends that some scholars have demonstrated that 1 Thess represents an earlier phase of Paul's theology and ethics and Gal, 1 & 2 Cor, Phil and Romans a second phase which cannot be harmonized with the first, needs to be addressed. Certainly, there is development in Paul's thought, and 1 Thess is signficantly different from Paul's other genuine epistles. However, the contention that the comparatively simple theology and ethics of 1 Thess cannot be harmonized with the more complex thought of the later letters is an exaggeration. The student need only remember that Paul's later thought adjusts and develops that which is earlier, but that the reverse is not true. To be sure, 1 Thess plays a comparatively minor role in this present book.

which relate directly to ethical or moral activity; it does not study the whole theological content of Paul's seven epistles. A further presupposition of this little book will be that when we speak of moral theology in Paul, as just explained, what we are really speaking of is Christian living. Any distinction between morality and Christian living in Paul's writings is simply out of place. To be sure, he writes for Christians.

The methodology used in this book is redactional criticism, which might more properly be called composition criticism. Whatever use Paul made of sources, the more basic and determinative factor is that he did compose these letters, even if they were dictated. His composition reveals his ideas and permits us to determine and to summarize his morality. Paul's use of sources is, of course, of interest, but it may not always be possible to determine exactly how he modified or nuanced a source. However, the very fact that he did take over a given source confirms his approval of its thought.

Frequently enough, one hears that Paul's letters were occasional and written to a local church or region to deal with particular concerns, and thus such letters should not be used to establish what the church today should do. But this observation repudiates the fact that the church has read and profited from Paul's letters for more than nineteen hundred years. These letters have had tremendous doctrinal and moral significance for Christians. Nonetheless, an effort will be made at the end of this volume to determine the relevance for us today of Paul's moral teaching. Up to that point, the assumption will be that what Paul writes applies to us, too.

The book is structured in the following manner. It falls into four parts. Part I reviews what Paul writes of God, Christ and the Spirit, and of what God has done in Christ as the reasons and sources of morality. Part II views Paul's moral directives to communities and individuals while Part III treats the way to live awaiting the Parousia, spiritual gifts, and Christian conduct. Finally, Part IV addresses the hermeneutical question of the relevance of Paul's moral teaching for today.

Scripture quotations are from the *Revised Standard Version*; these are modified only when judged to be incorrect or sexist.

I would be amiss if I did not thank a number of persons who were kind enough to help in the preparation of this book. Mrs. Elsie McGrath typed and proof-read a goodly portion of it. My good friends and colleagues, Frs. John J. Kilgallen, S.J. and William T. Miller, S.J., likewise read over the manuscript and made many useful suggestions. My thanks go also to my students and the faculty of the Department of Theological Studies of St. Louis University and to the Jesuit communities at St. Louis University and of the Pontifical Biblical Institute. I enjoyed the hospitality of the latter as I was finishing this undertaking. Professor Mary Ann Getty has been a patient and very supportive editor, and Mr. Michael Glazier, a creative and understanding publisher. Lastly, I thank the Danforth Foundation which funded the Second Danforth Chair in Humanities which I hold and which made possible my sabbatical endeavors.

I trust that in some way I have been able to clarify Paul's thought for the reader. His message has nourished my life for years; may the same experience and blessing be yours.

Part I

Sources of Morality

1

God, Christ and the Spirit: Reason and Source of Morality

For Paul, God achieves our salvation and thus leads us, in cooperation with him, to do good deeds (Rom 7:24-25). The source of everything and of every good action is God (1 Cor 3:21-23;4:7;8:6;15:28; Rom 8:28; Phil 2:13). Our ability to do good comes from him; that is why Paul says to the Philippians that he is sure God, "who began a good work in you will bring it to completion at the day of Jesus Christ" (Phil 1:6). God *works* a variety of activities in each of us (1 Cor 12:6). Consequently, human beings cannot boast except in what God has and is achieving in them (1 Cor 1:29;3:21; Rom 3:27;4:2).

Paul assures the Corinthians that the God of love and peace will be with them, so they ought to be at peace (2 Cor 13:11). Earlier, they were urged to keep order in their liturgical celebrations because God is not a God of confusion but of peace (1 Cor 14:33). Paul's wish for the Galatians is that God's grace and peace be with them (Gal 1:3) and for the Romans that the God of steadfastness and encouragement grant the Christians to think the same thing in Christ so that with one voice they might glorify God (Rom 15:6). God's peace surpasses all understanding and will keep the hearts and the minds of the Philippians in Christ Jesus (Phil 4:7). Always it is God who brings peace and harmony.

It is common knowledge that the verb, "to walk," looks to

moral living,[2] and in Romans (8:3-4) Paul maintains that God
has done what the law could not do. Through the Son, God
has condemned sin in the flesh in order that the just requirement of the law might be fulfilled in the Christians who walk
not according to the flesh but according to the Spirit. The
Christians can walk according to the Spirit because of what
God has done in Christ.

Paul wishes that God completely sanctify the Thessalonians
and keep their spirit, soul and body sound and blameless at
the coming of the Lord Jesus (1 Thess 5:23). In a similar vein,
God gives growth to the Corinthians; they are his field, his
building (1 Cor 3:6-9). He renews Paul's and his companions'
inner nature every day (2 Cor 4:16).

God's grace helps one act morally. Paul candidly admits
that God's grace has made him who he is and has permitted
him to work harder than all of the other apostles (1 Cor 15:10;
Rom 15:15). Paul begs the Corinthians not to have received
God's grace in vain (2 Cor 6:1), and then proceeds to imply
that they should put nothing in the way of their ministry but
rather commend themselves in every way. The Macedonians'
contribution to the collection for the poor is designated "the
grace of God" (2 Cor 8:1), and that of the Corinthians is
likewise attributed to God's grace (2 Cor 9:8,14). In each of the
above examples, God's grace brings about the good moral act.

In his interactions with the Corinthians, Paul claims to have
divine power which enables him to overcome obstacles to the
knowledge of God, and to take every thought captive to obey
Christ (2 Cor 10:4-6;6:7). Since the Corinthians already believe
in Christ, "to obey" in this passage looks to how the Corinthian
should live in Christ. However, it is God's power which a-
chieves this.

God leads Christians to comfort and to be reconciled to one

---

[2]Not infrequently, "to walk" is simply translated as "to live." For a thorough
consideration of "to walk," see Miguel Barriola, *El Espírito Santo y la praxis Cristiana:
El tema del camino en la teología de San Paolo* (Montevideo: Istituto Teológico del
Uruguay, 1977). Giuseppe Mollica ("La caritá comme cammino nel pensiero di San
Paolo," *Lateranum* 51 [1985] 83-7) directs our attention to the Pauline connection
between "to walk" and love.

another. God comforts Paul and Timothy in their afflictions in order that they might be able to comfort those who are afflicted. In fact, the comfort of God and of Paul are one and the same, and through Christ Paul and his companions share in it abundantly and pass it along to the Corinthians. Paul hopes that the Corinthians participate in this comfort which, according to the text, is received from God and shared with others (2 Cor 1:3-7).

Through Christ, God has reconciled Paul and Timothy to himself and given them the ministry of reconciliation. Actually, God in Christ was reconciling the world to himself, and he assigned to Paul and his companions the message of reconciliation. God makes his appeal through those who are ambassadors for Christ. So Paul beseeches the Corinthians to be reconciled (2 Cor 5:16-21). Surely, in this passage "reconciliation" is the equivalent of salvation. The Corinthians are called to realize this in action, and for Paul and Timothy it is a ministry, a message which they as ambassadors are to deliver. As noted elsewhere in Paul, God's kindness is meant to lead Christians to repentance (Rom 2:4).

Paul tells the Romans, "For in this hope we were saved" (Rom 8:24; cf. 8:18-25). The majestic passive, "were saved," reveals that this salvation and hope are due to God. Paul goes on to explain that one does not hope in what one sees. The thrust of the passage is that our hope comes from God, and yet is ours and gives meaning to our lives. Hope lets us wait in patience for the completion of God's saving activity.

Paul's ministry comes from God. God set him apart even before he was born and called him through his grace. Likewise, it pleased him to reveal his son to Paul in order that he might preach Christ among the Gentiles (Gal 1:15-16). According to the grace of God given him, Paul laid a foundation for the Christian life of each Corinthian (1 Cor 3:10). God has made him a competent minister of the new covenant, so Paul's confidence is from God, not from himself (2 Cor 3:4-6). Moreover, this latter passage is the only time that Paul clearly connects morality with the new covenant, which is not in a written code, but in the Spirit who gives life (but see 1 Cor 11:25). Paul's competent ministry of this new covenant is from God.

Even Paul's visits are attributable to God. For example, in his Letter to the Romans Paul prays that somehow by God's will he might be able to visit them. He hopes that it will be an opportunity to impart some spiritual gift to them, and that both he and they will be mutually encouraged by one another's faith (Rom 1:10-15; cf. 15:32). Paul wants to enjoy the Roman Christians' company and to be refreshed before he moves on to Spain (Rom 15:23-29,32). For Paul, this visit and its good results all will come about through God's will.

God gives the Christians victory over death through the Lord Jesus Christ (1 Cor 15:57). But this victory or triumph is not limited to death, nor should it be understood as only God's act. Rather, something happens in the Christians, and they live accordingly. Paul thanks God for leading him and his companions in triumph, for they are the aroma of Christ to God for spreading among those who are being saved, a fragrance from life to life (2 Cor 2:14-16). In a discussion of the things which might possibly separate us from the love of God, Paul's introductory observation is, "No, in all these things we are more than conquerors through him who loved us" (Rom 8:37).

God's victory over death affects our lives. Presently, we are anxious to be further clothed with life. We are of good courage and walk by faith. Whether we are "at home or away," we make it our aim to please God. Finally, each of us will have to appear before the judgment seat and receive good or evil, according to how each has lived (2 Cor 5:1-10; cf. Rom 2:16). The victory is God's, but it is also ours. Human action is significant, and we are responsible for what we do.

Christ as the Agent of Moral Activity

In the vast majority of situations, Paul writes that God the Father works *through* Christ. God executes salvation and every good *through* Christ. However, there are some passages in which Paul makes Christ the source of our morality. Let us now look at these passages.

A number of Pauline passages speak of the grace of Christ

(e.g. 2 Cor 13:14; Gal 1:3,6;6:18; Rom 16:20; Phil 1:2;4:23; Phlm 3,25), but these are not connected with moral activity. However, in a few others such a connection is to be found. Christ tells Paul, in prayer, "My grace is sufficient for you, for my power is made perfect in weakness." Consequently, Paul boasts of his weaknesses and is content with them as well as with insults, hardship and calamities, for he is strong with the power of Christ (2 Cor 12:8-10).

Paul generalizes about the grace of Christ in Rom 5:15-6:2. Grace abounds more than sin, and reigns through righteousness to eternal life through Jesus Christ our Lord. Everyone can have acquittal and life. Although this passage also uses the phrase, "*through* Christ," the direct bearing of his actions on us is noted. Moreover, the "reign in life" and "eternal life" do not only point to our resurrection. They relate to how we live our earthly lives, as the diatribe questions in Rom 6:1-2 (cf. v 15) make clear: "What shall we say then? Are we to continue in sin that grace may abound. By no means! How can we who died to sin still live in it?"

The power of Christ is mentioned elsewhere. Toward the end of 2 Cor (13:1-4), Paul speaks of his third visit to the Corinthians, from some of whom he fears opposition. He assures them that in any such encounter they will have proof of Christ speaking through him. Christ is powerfully in their midst; and Paul shares in this power, which is ultimately the Father's, for their benefit. In this passage Paul expands on his theology of weakness and relates it to dying and rising with Christ. Christ speaks through Paul, and through him he is powerful among the Corinthians.

It was indicated above that "life" for Paul is not limited to the afterlife. This is the case in Rom 8:10, "But if Christ is in you, although your bodies are dead because of sin, your spirits are alive because of righteousness." Earlier (v 4), the passage reads, ". . . in order that the just requirement of the law might be fulfilled in us, who *walk* not according to the flesh but according to the Spirit." What Christ can do for a Christian finds lofty expression in Gal 2:20: "I have been crucified with Christ; it is no longer I who live, but Christ who lives in me; and the life I now live in the flesh I live by faith in the Son of

God, who loved me and gave himself for me." Christ totally permeates and affects Paul's whole life.

Christ sets us free (Gal 5:1; cf. Rom 8:2), and so Paul instructs the Galatians to stand fast and not again submit to the yoke of slavery. That this freedom looks to moral action is demonstrated by v 13 of the same chapter: "For you were called to freedom, brethren; only do not use your freedom as an opportunity for the flesh, but through love be servants of one another." Christ frees the Galatians for love and service of one another.

Two other passages report actions that Christ works in Paul. Christ has made Paul his own. This enables Paul to press on since he has not already obtained the resurrection of the dead nor is he already perfect. He forgets what lies behind and strains toward what lies ahead (Phil 3:12-16). The passage does contain the words, "I press on toward the goal for the prize of the upward call of God in Christ Jesus," but this should be viewed as another way of saying Christ has made Paul his own. However, the very fact that Paul can write the latter means that he in part begins to predicate things of Christ as he does of the Father. Also important for the scope of this book is Paul's description of the moral effect of his being seized by Christ, "Only let us hold true to what we have attained" (v 16).

In Romans we find Paul's explanation:

> For I will not venture to speak of anything except what Christ has wrought through me to win obedience from the Gentiles, by word and deed, by the power of signs and wonders, by the power of the Holy Spirit, so that from Jerusalem and as far round as Illyricum I have fully preached the gospel of Christ, ... (15:18-19).

In this pericope Christ has made Paul a preacher and a miracle worker. Again, Christ is seen as an agent of moral activity.

The Holy Spirit as an Agent of Moral Activity

The Holy Spirit plays a significant part in Paul's overall view of morality, and the Spirit is seen as an agent of morality.[3] The variety of gifts are due to the Spirit, and they are given for the common good. "All these are inspired by one and the same Spirit, who apportions to each one individually as he wills" (1 Cor 12:11; cf. vv 4-10).

Christian fellowship is also predicated of the Spirit (2 Cor 13:13), basically because by the Spirit we are baptized into the one body of Christ (1 Cor 12:12-13). As the rest of 1 Cor 12 testifies, this fellowship calls Christians to recognize one another's gifts and to be accepting of one another. Later, Paul urges the Philippians that if, among other things, there is any participation in the Spirit, they are to complete his joy by being of one mind, having the same love and being in full accord (Phil 2:1f).

The Spirit helps Christians in their weakness, for they do not know how to pray as they ought (Rom 8:26-27). The Spirit intercedes for the saints according to God's will. Paul's implication is that this intercession is heard because God knows what is the Spirit's mind. Thus, the Spirit affects the prayer of Christians and renders it efficacious before the Father who, in the final analysis, controls everything.

We have seen that the Holy Spirit brings about unity and fellowship among the Christians; and the various gifts of the members of the community flow from the Spirit, embrace the whole of Christian existence and are to be used for the common good. Likewise, it was noted that the Spirit helps Christians in their weaknesses because they do not pray as they ought.

Paul connects the Spirit with morality in other ways. Exactly how one ought to designate this further activity of the Spirit in Christian moral living may be more difficult than

---

[3]See J-N. Aletti, "L'ethicisation de l'Esprit Saint: Foi et éthos dans épitres pauliniennes," *Ethique, religion et foi* (sous la direction de J. Doré; Travaux de l'U.R.E. de théologie et de sciences religieuses: Le point théologique 43; Paris: Beauchesne, 1985) 123-142; P. Perkins, "Paul and Ethics," *Int* 38 (1984) 268-80.

indicating the examples of it. Ultimately, it comes to God's working in us through the Spirit.

Paul contrasts the Spirit and flesh (1 Cor 3:1-4; Gal 5:16-25;6:8; Rom 8:1-17). Different desires arise in us depending on whether we are led by the Spirit or by the flesh. To set the mind on the flesh is death, but to set the mind on the Spirit is life and peace. Important for our present study is that the terminology used about the Holy Spirit's activity shows that it bears on Christian moral living. Paul instructs the Galatians "to walk" by the Spirit (Gal 5:16; cf. Rom 8:4-6), and not to gratify the desires of the flesh. If they walk by the Spirit they should have no conceit, no provoking of one another, no envy of one another (Gal 5:25-26; cf. 1 Cor 3:3-4). They are "led" by the Spirit and so are not under the law (Gal 5:18; Rom 8:14), or as Paul also phrases it, "For the law of the Spirit of life in Christ Jesus has set me free from the law of sin and death" (Rom 8:2).[4] If by the spirit they put to death the deeds of the body they will live; their own spirits are alive (Rom 8:10-11,13). Certainly, Paul held that the Holy Spirit was our guarantee of eternal life (e.g. Rom 8:14-17,22-25; cf. 2 Cor 1:22;5:5), but to live in the Spirit likewise determines how we are to act now.

The Spirit relates to wisdom and discernment. When Paul speaks of the wisdom of God versus human wisdom, he launches into a discussion of the Spirit. For Paul, the Spirit comprehends God's thoughts and assists Sosthenes and Paul in understanding the gifts God has bestowed on them. The unspiritual do not receive the gifts of God; to them these gifts are folly and cannot be understood because they are spiritually discerned. Paul then continues (and leaves no doubt that he is relating the Spirit not only to salvation but to moral activity) that he cannot address the Corinthians as spiritual. They are still in the flesh since there is jealousy and strife among them.

---

[4]For an understanding of the Pauline relationship between law and the Spirit, the reader is referred to Eckhart Reinmuth, *Geist und Gesetz: Studien zu Voraussetzungen und Inhalt der paulinischen Paränese* (ed. T. Holtz *et al.*; Theologische Arbeiten 44; Berlin: Evangelische, 1985).

They are arguing about whether they belong "to Paul" or "to Apollos" (1 Cor 2:10-3:4; cf. 1:1). Paul writes of the fruits of the Spirit. They are love (cf. Rom 15:30), joy, peace, patience, kindness, goodness, faithfulness, gentleness and self-control (Gal 5:22-24). All of these pertain to Christian living in this world, yet are attributed to the Spirit. The Spirit enables us to so live and to crucify the flesh with its passions and desires.

According to Paul, the Holy Spirit is the source of other moral activity. In 1 Thess 4:7-8 (cf. Ezek 36:26f;37:14), we read, "For God has not called us for uncleanness, but in holiness. Therefore, whoever disregards this, disregards not man but God, who gives his Holy Spirit to you." There are only a limited number of possible interpretations of these two verses. The Holy Spirit assists us in knowing what is holy, and if we reject that insight we reject God who gave us the Spirit, or the Spirit enables us to live a life of holiness, or a combination of both of these. Whichever of these interpretations is accepted, Paul has associated the Holy Spirit with moral activity.

We find the expression, "be aglow with the Spirit," in Rom 12:11. First of all, this expression appears in the imperative section of the letter. In the imperative sections of his letters Paul calls the respective community to certain actions which should follow from the sections of the letters where Paul teaches what Christians hold on given points. Moreover, the immediate context of "be aglow with the Spirit" is, "Never flag in zeal, be aglow with the Spirit, serve the Lord." Prior to this Paul asks for genuine love, the hating of evil and clinging to the good, and mutual concern. Afterwards, he instructs the Romans to rejoice in hope, to be patient in tribulation and constant in prayer, to contribute to the needs of the saints and practice hospitality. Consequently, "Be aglow with the Spirit" is a description of a Christian's moral life; the Spirit gives vitality to this life.

The Spirit also produces in the Christian the right reaction to someone who has been found trespassing. The spiritual person restores him or her with gentleness, and reflects that, since temptation can touch anyone, alertness is appropriate for everyone (Gal 6:1).

Prayer and Morality

Given Paul's emphasis on God as the source of everything, it is not surprising that prayer appears as a means of enlisting God's help so that human beings act morally. Or to put it another way, ultimately prayer is just another way of saying that all depends on God. Of course, prayer itself is a moral act. Normally, Paul begins a letter with a thanksgiving for what God has done for the addressees. He likewise calls his readers to prayer (e.g. 1 Thess 5:17,23; Phil 1:19; Phlm 22). He tells the Thessalonians that Silvanus, Titus and he himself cannot sufficiently thank God for them and the joy they feel because of them. Paul and his companions pray further that they might see the Thessalonians face to face and supply whatever is lacking to their faith (1 Thess 3:9-10). Apparently, Paul believes that God has brought about the Thessalonians' positive reception of Timothy and his companions and that, thanks to prayer, God may also occasion their visit and prosper their apostolic effort with the Thessalonians.

Paul prays that the Corinthians do no wrong, but improve (2 Cor 13:7-9). Earlier the prayers of the Corinthians and others (2 Cor 1:8-11) were the source of a blessing for Paul in Asia. The context reveals that this blessing kept Paul from being crushed by his affliction and made him rely on God and hope in him for deliverance. Paul, in a similar passage, asks the Roman Christians to pray that he be delivered from the unbeliever in Judea and that his service (the collection) be acceptable to the saints in Jerusalem, that he might with joy visit the Romans and be refreshed (Rom 15:30-32).

Twice, in the Letter to the Philippians, Paul relates prayer to moral activity. In the thanksgiving (Phil 1:3-11), Paul is grateful to God because of the Philippians' partnership in the gospel, "And I am sure that he who began a good work in you will bring it to completion on the day of Jesus Christ." His prayer continues, "that your love may abound more and more, ... that you may approve what is excellent, and may be pure and blameless for the day of Christ, filled with the fruits of righteousness which come through Jesus Christ,..." Later, in the same letter (4:6-7), Paul instructs the Philippians to have

no anxiety but in everything through prayer to make their
requests known to God, "and the peace of God, which surpasses all understanding, will keep your hearts and minds in
Christ Jesus." Christian prayer calms anxiety and transmits
peace.

The thanksgiving of the Letter to Philemon likewise concerns prayer and moral activity (Phlm 4-7). Paul thanks God
because of Philemon's love and faith. God has caused Paul
much joy and comfort because Philemon has refreshed the
hearts of the Christians who gather at his home.

In this chapter, we have seen that for Paul the Father,
Christ and the Holy Spirit can all be designated as sources of
morality.[5] However, Paul usually writes of God the Father as
the one who achieves and accomplishes every good. Prayer is
the recognition of this overall reality.

---

[5]Further treatment of this topic can be found in C. Spicq, *Vie morale et Trinité
Sainte selon Saint Paul* (LD 19; Paris: Cerf, 1957) 25-71. He does not limit his
consideration to "Paul's genuine epistles." Also, he includes in his treatment of Christ
the Christian's unity with him (pp. 34-47).

2

What God Has Done in Christ as a Source of Morality

Paul is thoroughly consistent in his contention that God in Christ brings about our salvation and moral activity. Up to this point we have seen that Paul can make the Father, Christ or the Holy Spirit all sources of human morality. Let us now look at the variety of ways that Paul writes of how human morality finds its source in what God has done in Christ.

The Unity of Christians with Christ and Morality

Paul's main way of speaking about salvation is the unity of the Christian with Christ. The fact is that Paul has any number of terms for salvation. Almost everyone is acquainted with "expiation," "reconciliation," "redemption" ("bought with a price"), "righteousness" ("justification"), and "salvation." But in any complete treatment of salvation in Paul, a number of other expressions have to be considered, such as: "gospel," "promise," "blessing," "beloved," "called," "chosen," "foreknown," "consolation" ("comfort"), "freedom," "glorify," "grace," "adopted sons and daughters," "heirs," "life," "predestined," "resurrection," "sanctified" ("sanctification," "made holy," "saint"), "washed" and "wisdom" ("knowledge," "thinking"). Our concern in this book is that Paul has linked Christian morality with salvation, even though there is a tendency to view Paul's soteriology rigidly and thus to separate it from moral activity or "good works." Nonetheless, for Paul Christian living and morality flow from what God has done in Christ. At times, a Pauline concept can from one point of view indicate salvation, and from another a human action achieved through God's grace. We attempt to maintain clarity on exact meanings, and our major concern is to make available to the reader the Pauline data on morality, and on salvation only in so far as it bears on his notion of morality or Christian living.

Of course, the Christian's unity with Christ is due to the Father (cf. 1 Cor 1:9,30). The most obvious result is that Christians are to actualize this unity with Christ.[6] We are one body (1 Cor 12:12-31; Rom 12:3-8), but many members with different functions and gifts. This diversity has to be recognized, and our gifts are to be used for the benefit of one another. We are to desire the higher gifts. Yet the weaker members are indispensable, and those who lack honor or beauty deserve greater recognition and respect. No one should have too high an opinion of himself or herself, but should rather make balanced judgments in accord with God's gifts. Racial, social and sexual distinctions disappear; at least, they are to be subordinated to our unity in Christ (Gal 3:26-28). Whatever happens to one of us happens to all of us, for we are one body and care for one another (cf. Gal 6:1f). The collection for the poor in Jerusalem is a manifestation of this (Gal 2:10; cf. 1 Cor 16:1-4; 2 Cor 8-9; Rom 15:25-31).

---

[6]For example, for the importance of the unity of the Christian with Christ for Paul's morality, see F. Pastor-Ramos, "La ética paulina—El fundamento de la vida cristiana según San Pablo," *Moralia* 6 (1984) 129-44; E. P. Sanders, *Paul and Palestinian Judaism: A Comparison of Patterns of Religion* (Philadelphia: Fortress, 1977) 438-40,453-70,502-8,514,520-3; H. Schürmann, "Haben die paulinischen Wertungen und Weisungen Modellcharacter? Beobachtungen und Anmerkungen zur Frage nach ihrer formalen Eigenart und inhaltlichen Verbindlichkeit," *Greg* 56 (1975) 245; A. Schweitzer, *Die Mystik des Apostels Paulus* (Tübingen, J. C. B.. Mohr, 1930) 285-89. Interestingly, on the basis of Gal 3:8f,14, A. J. M. Wedderburn ("Some observations on Paul's Use of the Phrases 'in Christ' and 'with Christ'," *JSNT* 25 [1985] 83-97) suggests a background in which Abraham and Christ are viewed as representative figures through whom God acts toward the human race: he acts toward them "in" these figures and they are caught up "with them" in that divine initiative of grace.

Our unity with Christ means that there should be no dissensions among us. This is Paul's appeal to the Corinthians who are dividing themselves according to who baptized them. They should be united in the same mind and have the same judgment (cf. 1 Cor 1:10-13). Their jealousy and strife demonstrate that they are still of the flesh (1 Cor 3:3). Whether Euodia and Syntyche are the source of division among the Philippians or not, they are exhorted by Paul to agree in the Lord (Phil 4:2), as is the whole community (2:2; cf. 2:1-11). Likewise, it is contrary to the truth of the gospel to decide who will eat with whom on the basis of circumcision (Gal 2:11-14). Needless to say, such a divisive decision would have established two classes of Christians, the elite (the circumcised) and the uncircumcised.

Our unity with Christ gives us a new self-image. Basic psychology informs us that it is our self-image that determines what we do, and this insight obviously has validity on the theological level. We have just seen how the image of the body of Christ bears on Christian living. This and other images for unity serve Paul as he exhorts the Corinthians not to have relations with temple prostitutes (1 Cor 6:12-20). Sexuality should not be viewed as if it were another human activity like eating. According to Paul, the Corinthians are members of Christ and so cannot become members of a prostitute. Of course, he bases this reasoning on Gen 2:24, "The two shall become one flesh." Moreover, immorality is a sin against one's own body, which is a temple of the Holy Spirit and belongs to God who bought us with a price. The body is not meant for immorality, but for the Lord and for the resurrection. Unity with Christ has given the Corthinians a new self-image, and they should so live.

Paul writes in 2 Cor 5:14-18 that if anyone is in Christ, he or she is a new creation. The old has passed away and the new has come, and all of this is from God. Consequently, we have to view one another in a different perspective and overcome our selfishness. Christ's love now controls us because we know that he died for all of us. In fact, we died with him, and now we live for him and no longer for ourselves. The "new creation" theme appears again in Gal 6:14-16 and serves as a rule by which Christians are to live: "For neither circumcision counts for anything, nor uncircumcision, but a new creation. Peace and mercy be upon all who walk by this rule, upon the Israel of God."

A number of Pauline passages specify the Christian's unity in dying and rising with Christ. Some of these join this union to moral living. Perhaps the most relevant passage here is Rom 6 (cf. 5:12-21; 7:1-6). Our dying and rising with Christ in baptism should have the following results in us:[7]

> We too might walk in newness of life (6:4) ... We know that our old self was crucified with him so that the sinful body might be destroyed, and we might no longer be enslaved to sin, ... But if we have die with Christ, we believe that we shall also live with him (6:6,8; cf. 5:17-18;6:1-2,12-18), ... So you also must consider yourself dead to sin and alive to God in Christ Jesus (6:11; cf. v 23).

The general context leaves the reader in no doubt that "life" in these verses refers not only to the resurrection but to moral living in this world. Actually, Rom 6:4 itself is sufficiently clear on this point. However, Rom 6:19 reads, "For just as you once yielded your members to impurity and to greater and greater iniquity, so now yield your members to righteousness for sanctification," and Rom 6:22, "But now that you have been set free from sin and have become slaves of God, the return you get is sanctification and its end, eternal life." Finally, Rom 7:4 states, "Likewise, my brethren, you have died to the law through the body of Christ, so that you may belong to another, to him who has been raised from the dead in order that we

---

[7] Hans Halter (*Taufe und Ethos: Paulinische Kriterien für das Proprium christlicher Moral,* Freiburger theologischen Studien; Freiburg; Herder, 1977, 103-82,304-84,409-92) rightly holds that the theological, christological, eschatological and spiritual existence grounded in baptism is the basis for Christian morality or ethics. He studies 1 Cor 1:10-17;6:1-11;10:1-13;12:12f; 2 Cor 1:12-22; Gal 2:15-21;3:26-29;5:13-25; Rom 6:1-23;7:1-6 and a number of passages from Colossians and Ephesians. Confer C. Spicq, *Vie morale et Trinité Sainte,* 81-9 and S. Zedda, *Relativo e assoluto nella morale di San Paolo* (Biblioteca di cultura religiosa 43; Brescia, Paideia, 1984) 33-39.

may bear fruit for God," which Paul designates "the new life of the Spirit" (Rom 7:6).

Paul reflects in his Letter to the Philippians on how dying and rising with Christ have become part of his own life. He makes sense out of his own sufferings because he sees them as sharing in Christ's and becoming like him in death. According to the context, Paul has subordinated everything to this knowing of Christ (Phil 3:7-11).

At times, Paul stresses the dying with Christ. His explanation of how he puts up with the daily demands of his ministry is: "Henceforth let no man trouble me; for I bear on my body the marks of Jesus" (Gal 6:17).[8] In addition, belonging to Christ calls the Christian to crucify the flesh with its passions and desires (Gal 5:24; Rom 13:11-14). Union with the death of Christ enables the Christian to bear difficulties and suffering, and calls for discipline and living one's new self-image. Perhaps the highest verbal expression of overcoming one's less noble self and dying with Christ is: "I have been crucified with Christ; it is no longer I who live, but Christ who lives in me; and the life I now live in the flesh I live by faith in the Son of God, who loved me and gave himself for me" (Gal 2:20).

Elsewhere, Paul claims that he and his companions always carry in their bodies the death of Jesus, whether it be affliction, perplexity, persecution, being struck down or whatever, so that the life of Jesus may also be manifested in them. Apparently this is all for the sake of the ministry because Paul concludes this paragraph with the words, "So death is at work in us, but life in you" (2 Cor 4:12; cf. 4:1,8-11).

Even though Christ has made him his own, Paul does not think that he has already won the race; but he forgets the past and strains forward to what lies ahead. He asserts that anyone who is mature will have the same conviction, and a few verses later he adds, "Brothers and sisters, join in imitating me, and mark those who so live as you have an example in us" (Phil

---

[8]H. D. Betz, *Galatians: A Commentary on Paul's Letter to the Churches in Galatia* (Hermeneia; Philadelphia: Fortress, 1979) 323-25.

3:17; cf. 3:11-16). Unity with Christ has not made Paul complacent, but challenged him to keep right on going until he reaches the resurrection of the dead.

The Christians' unity with Christ calls for certain actions. In Christ neither circumcision nor uncircumcision is of any avail, but faith working through love (Gal 5:6). Union with Christ can also make one bold; Paul's union could render him bold enough to command Philemon how to treat Onesimus. However, his love moves him to appeal to, rather than command him (Phlm 8-9).

Union with Christ demands that the Christian shun the worship of idols. The cup of blessing which we bless is a participation in the blood of Christ, and the bread which we break is a participation in the body of Christ. Because there is one bread, we who are many are one body, for we all partake of the one bread. We cannot drink the cup of the Lord and the cup of demons. We cannot partake of the table of the Lord and the table of demons (1 Cor 10:14-21). The risen Lord in the Eucharist unifies us, our participation in any other sacred meal would mean our union with the idols (demons) in whose honor it is offered.

Paul uses his central theological interest, the union of the Christian with Christ, to express his deep feeling and concern for his fellow Jews. In Rom 9:1-5 Paul solemnly contends, "I am speaking the truth *in Christ*, I am not lying, my conscience bears me witness in the Holy Spirit," and then goes on to explain "my great sorrow" and the "unceasing anguish in my heart." He could wish that he himself was accursed and cut off from Christ for the sake of the Jews, his brothers and sisters, those related to him by race. Paul here speaks out of his union with Christ, and at the same time he employs that union to stress the tremendous significance he gives to concern for other Jews. Certainly, Paul is using an hyperbole and expressing a wish, and nothing he could have done would have determined how the Jews reacted to Christ. Nonetheless, the moral import of Paul's hyperbole for the Christian stance toward Jews is not to be missed.

Righteousness (Justification)

Justification or righteousness is primarily God's action (e.g. Rom 1:17;3:21-26,30;8:30,33; 1 Cor 6:11; Gal 3:8), although Paul also writes that through the obedience of Christ many will be made righteous (Rom 5:19). Probably because of his emphasis on justification by faith alone, not by works, Paul does not often draw a connection between righteousness and Christian living or moral action. But, at times, he does. Of course, the righteous person lives by faith (Gal 3:11; Rom 1:17; cf. ch. 4 below). One way that Paul commends his ministry to everyone is "with the weapons of righteousness for the right hand and for the left" (2 Cor 6:7). The reference must be to certain things Paul does in his ministry. More generally, the Roman Christians are told that they were set free from sin and have become slaves of righteousness, so now they yield their members to righteousness for sanctification (Rom 6:18-20; cf v 13). In his exhortation to the Corinthians to contribute to the collection, Paul includes the statement that God will increase the harvest of their righteousness (2 Cor 9:10). Surely, God increases the harvest, but the Corinthians themselves are going to make a contribution because of their righteousness. Paul assures the Galatians that through the Spirit, by faith, they wait for the hope of righteousness (Gal 5:5). Righteousness in this text gives us grounds for hope. Finally, Paul prays that the love of the Philippians may abound more and more, with knowledge and discernment, so that they may approve what is excellent and may be pure and blameless for the day of Christ, filled with the fruits of righteousness which come through Jesus Christ (Phil 1:9-11). The "fruits of righteousness" surely come through Jesus Christ, but they likewise designate good actions the Philippians will have performed. Righteousness or justification, then, calls for our moral living.

The Gospel, Faith, Grace, Promises and Freedom and Morality

Since Paul wrote before the formation of any of our present gospels, "gospel" for him means that which he preaches. To be sure, the gospel is the power of God for salvation to everyone who has faith (Rom 1:16-17), and it leads the Christian to definite actions. When Paul speaks of his ministry and asserts that he has become all things to everyone that he might by all means save some, he explains, "I do it all for the sake of the gospel, that I might share in its blessings" (1 Cor 9:22f). Earlier, in the same chapter (v 12; cf. 2 Cor 6:3), he phrases it, "but we endure anything rather than put an obstacle in the way of the gospel of Christ." The truth of Paul's gospel is freedom from slavery, and there are to be no divisions because of dietary laws (Gal 2:4f,14).

Paul instructs the Philippians that the manner of their life ought to be worthy of the gospel of Christ. Whether he is absent or present, he wants to hear of them that they stand firm in one spirit, with one mind, striving side by side for the faith of the gospel and not at all frightened by their opponents. Not only has it been granted to them to believe in Christ, but to suffer for his sake (Phil 1:27-30). The gospel of Christ affects how the Philippians live and the unity they should preserve among themselves. All of this is a clear omen of their salvation.

When Paul is approaching the Corinthians about their contribution to the collection for the poor in Jerusalem, he has the following to say, "Under the test of this service, you will glorify God by your obedience in acknowledging the gospel of Christ, and by the generosity of your contribution for them and for all others" (2 Cor 9:13). The collection is called "a service," and the Corinthians' sharing in it is an obedient recognition of the gospel. Teaching, too, can be the equivalent of Paul's gospel and so function as a directive for moral actions (Rom 6:17; 16:17).

To be closely associated with Paul's gospel is faith; at times it can mean the same as gospel. Whatever does not proceed from faith is sin, and if anyone doubts about whether or not he or she is permitted to eat something but still eats it, they are condemned because they did not act from faith (Rom 14:23). All Christian morality flows from faith.

At times, "grace" for Paul is the equivalent of salvation. In a number of instances, grace leads to moral activity. Right after he states that God, who raised the Lord Jesus, will raise Paul and Timothy with him and bring them and the Corinthians into his presence, Paul continues, "so that as grace extends to more and more people it may increase thanksgiving, to the glory of God" (2 Cor 4:13-15). In this passage grace is to be identified with the message of the resurrection of Jesus, Timothy, Paul and the Corinthians; as it spreads, this grace increases thanksgiving. Paul does view his vision and apostleship as grace (Gal 1:15f; Rom 1:5;12:3;15:15f), and he entreats the Corinthians not to accept the grace of God in vain (2 Cor 6:1). This latter exhortation follows a famous passage on reconciliation and precedes one on ministry.

In 2 Cor 8:9 Paul writes of the grace of our Lord Jesus Christ, who though he was rich, yet for the sake of the Corinthians became poor, so that by his poverty they might become rich. This grace of Jesus serves as a motivation for the Corinthians to take a generous part in the collection for the poor in Jerusalem, which collection is called "the grace of God" (2 Cor 8:1) and "this gracious work" (vv 6,7,19). The grace of salvation should lead the Corinthians to do this gracious work for the poor in Jerusalem.

Earlier, when the unity of the Christian with Christ and its relevance for morality were addressed, attention was called to Rom 5:15-21 among other passages, and evidence was offered that "life" in the passages referred not only to the resurrection but to moral living. However, "grace" likewise appears in these verses (Rom 5:15-17,20-21; 6:1-2,14-15; cf. 3:5-8), and so again has to do with morality.

Paul has connected promises with moral activity. He writes the Corinthians, "Since we have these promises, beloved, let us cleanse ourselves from every defilement of body and spirit, and make holiness perfect in the fear of God" (2 Cor 7:1). Whether this verse is from Paul or whether it comes from some earlier source, it does stand in his letter and points to the conviction that God's promises move Christians to personal holiness. Furthermore, the new covenant, which is the equivalent of the promise, is of the Spirit and gives life (2 Cor 3:6; cf. Gal 3:15-20).

Freedom, for Paul, means that we Christians are no longer in bondage to sin but rather to God and righteousness. Formerly the Galatians were in bondage to beings which were not gods; they are not to turn back again to these weak and beggarly elemental spirits. Nor should they observe days, months, seasons or years (Gal 4:8-10). Christian freedom means that this past bondage is to be permanently rejected, and one should not follow the desires of the flesh. Rather, Christian freedom through love leads us to be servants of one another. In fact, the whole law is fulfilled in the words, "You shall love your neighbor as yourself." Since this is so, our freedom can be limited by the conscience of another (1 Cor 10:28-29). Certainly, Christian freedom is not characterized by biting and devouring one another, which only provokes others to give the same treatment (Gal 5:13-15). Our freedom from sin means that we now yield ourselves to righteousness for sanctification, whose end is eternal life (Rom 6:18-19). Christians are free to serve God and righteousness, to love and serve one another and to be holy.[9]

Wisdom, Knowledge and Thinking and Pauline Morality

Wisdom and knowledge bear on Christian conduct. God and the Spirit are their source,[10] and Christ is called the wisdom

[9]For further discussion of Christian freedom in Paul, the reader can refer to Ignace de la Potterie & Stanislaus Lyonnet *La vie selon l'Esprit: Condition du chrétiens* (Paris, Cerf, 1965) 169-95. However, Lyonnet in his treatment of the topic does not limit himself to what we have called "Paul's genuine epistles." Also, his tendency to argue from the whole of the New Testament does not always seem justified. See likewise C. Spicq, *Vie morale et Trinité Sainte,* 56-58.

[10]For God as the source of wisdom or knowledge, see 1 Cor 1:21-24,30; 2:6-9; Rom 11:33-35; 16:27; for the Spirit, 1 Cor 2:4,10-18. Above we spoke of wisdom and the Spirit, p. 24.

of God (1 Cor 1:24; cf. v 30). "Knowledge" can be used by Paul as just cognitional awareness, but often enough he joins it to the gospel or some related truth, or to some human perception, all of which have relevance for Christian living or morality. The human qualities of wisdom, knowledge and thinking are gifts of the Spirit and principles of human activity (1 Cor 10:14f;12:8;16:15f; Rom 16:19). These gifts, however, are to be subordinated to love (1 Cor 8:1;13:2; cf. vv 8f).

Although knowledge can puff up, it is interrelated with discernment and really should lead to good actions.[11] In baptism, Christian knowledge realizes that death no longer reigns over Christ, and that we are baptized into his death. We died to sin and so are no longer enslaved to it (Rom 6:3,6,9). Even pagans know God, though they do not honor him (Rom 1:20-23; cf. Gal 4:19). In fact, all humankind should have known the way of peace, but they were all sinners (Rom 3:17).

Paul speaks with the wisdom of God (1 Cor 2:1-9; 2 Cor 1:12), for his wisdom is not of this world (1 Cor 1:18-30;3:18-20). Like a wise master builder, Paul lays a foundation on which someone else builds (1 Cor 3:10). He knows that, as a proclaimer of the gospel, he has a right to be supported by the Corinthians, but he wants to make the gospel available free of charge (1 Cor 9:13-18). Paul's knowledge, that God will raise us with Jesus and bring us into his presence, results in his belief and proclamation (2 Cor 4:13f). A few verses later he writes, "Therefore, knowing the fear of the Lord, we persuade everyone..." (2 Cor 5:11). In everything, Paul commends himself as a servant of God "by purity, knowledge,..." (2 Cor 6:6).

Paul knows that, through the Philippians' prayers and the help of the Spirit of Jesus Christ, his imprisonment will turn out for his deliverance (Phil 1:19). Further, he knows that he will remain and continue with them, for their progress and joy in faith (1:25). More centrally, the surpassing worth of knowing Jesus Christ, his Lord, has led Paul to count everything else as loss (3:8).

---

[11]See 1 Cor 8:1-11; Rom 2:18;13:11-14; Phil 1:9b-11; Phlm 6.

Knowledge, or an equivalent expression, can be tied to a particular moral action. The Thessalonians should know how to treat a wife (4:2,4f). Their knowledge of those who labor among them, and are over them in the Lord and admonish them, should lead to love and esteem (5:12-13). The Corinthians know that they are God's temple, and that the Spirit of God dwells in them. If anyone destroys God's temple, God will destroy him or her (1 Cor 3:16f). Likewise, the Corinthians should learn not to go beyond what is written, lest some one of them be puffed up (1 Cor 4:6). Moreover, there ought to be some one among them wise enough to judge the grievances that they are bringing before pagan judges (1 Cor 6:1-8). On a more personal level, their knowledge that their bodies are members of Christ, that he who joins himself to a prostitute becomes one body with her, and that their bodies are temples of the Holy Spirit within them, should help them avoid sexual relationships with the temple prostitutes (1 Cor 6:15f,19). Besides, it is common knowledge that in a race all run, but only one receives the prize. So, the Corinthians are to run to obtain it (1 Cor 9:24). Likewise, they should understand how to dress (1 Cor 11:3). More importantly, they know that as they have shared in Paul's sufferings, they will also share in his comfort (2 Cor 1:7; cf. 1 Thess 3:3f; Rom 5:3). Now the Corinthians know no one from a human point of view; everyone is a new creation in Christ. There follows, in Paul's text, a call to reconciliation (2 Cor 5:16-20). The Corinthians' knowledge of God's grace among the Macedonians, and of Christ's becoming poor, although he was rich, calls them to complete their contribution to the collection (2 Cor 8:1,9). Wisdom can be used ironically (e.g. 1 Cor 4:10; 2 Cor 11:19), but these usages, too, are in contexts which call the Corinthians to more Christian behavior.

Since some Philippians know that Paul is in prison for the defense of the gospel, they preach Christ out of love (Phil 1:15f). Lastly, and by way of a summary, Paul says to the Philippians, "What you have learned and received and heard and seen in me, do" (Phil 4:9).

Thinking, too, leads to moral action. Obviously, different ways of thinking are appropriate to different times in one's life

(1 Cor 13:9-12). However, those who live according to the Spirit set their minds on things of the Spirit (Rom 8:5; contrast Phil 3:19). More practically, Paul bids the Roman Christians not to think more highly of themselves than is right (Rom 12:3; cf. v 16;11:25); to preserve harmony in his communities, he urged Christians to think the same thing (2 Cor 13:11; Phil 2:2,5;3:15;4:2; Rom 12:16;15:5f). When he speaks of the weak in the community, Paul reflects on personal responsibility and sets the following norm: "He or she, who thinks a day deserves special observance, thinks this to honor the Lord"(Rom 14:6). Lastly, Paul is grateful for the revived thoughts of the Philippians on his behalf; to be sure, the Philippians always thought this way, but there was no opportunity to express this (Phil 4:10).

After words which indicate knowledge, Paul can give what might be classified as a proverbial statement. These statements can be general or specific, and they always at least imply how Christians ought to live. According to Paul, the Corinthians know that in the Lord their labor is not in vain (1 Cor 15:58), or as he states it elsewhere, "We know that in everything God works for good with those who love him, who are called according to his purpose" (Rom 8:28). Likewise, the Roman Christians should know that they are slaves of the one they obey—either of sin, which leads to death, or of obedience, which leads to life (Rom 6:16; cf. Gal 4:8-9).

Pauline Morality and the Resurrection, Parousia and Judgment

Paul's teachings on the resurrection, Parousia and judgment furnish moral directives.[12] Earlier, under the rubric of "dying and rising with Christ," the relationship between the resurrection and morality was discussed. It is again noted here to give a context to Parousia and Judgment and to view an additional passage. Because Paul looks to the things that are

---

[12]C. Spicq, *Vie morale et Trinité Sainte*, 81-89.

unseen and eternal, he does not lose heart but views the present reality as a slight momentary affliction which prepares him for the glory which is beyond all comparison. Now he groans, is in anxiety and longs to be further clothed. But he is always of good courage and walks by faith. In all this, Paul makes it his aim to please God (2 Cor 4:16-5:10).

The Parousia, the day of the Lord, and judgment foresee good deeds on the part of the Christian. When anyone pays us a visit, we make preparations. The Parousia is like a visit. We must be ready, when the Lord comes, and not be found unprepared, sleeping or as sons and daughters of the night. Likewise, the Parousia, or day of the Lord, is often associated with judgment and so Christians can be held responsible for the good or evil that they did during their lives on earth.

Paul first addresses the question of the Parousia, or the day of the Lord, in 1 Thessalonians. Christians from Macedonia and Achaia report what a welcome Paul and his companions had among the Thessalonians, who turned from idols to serve a living and true God and to wait for his Son from heaven (1 Thess 1:8-10). Paul prays that the Lord may help them to increase and abound in love for one another and for everyone, just as Paul and his companions do for them, and that he may establish their hearts blameless in holiness before God the Father at the coming of the Lord Jesus with all his saints (1 Thess 3:11-12;5:23). The day of the Lord will come like a thief in the night, but the Thessalonians are not in darkness so they should not be surprised. They are not to sleep, as others do, but to be awake and sober, to put on the breastplate of faith and love and, for a helmet, the hope of salvation. They are not destined for wrath, but for salvation through our Lord Jesus Christ. He died for them that they, whether awake or asleep, might live with him. Consequently, they are to continue doing what they have been doing, encouraging and building up one another (1 Thess 5:1-11).

In his thanksgiving in 1 Cor 1:4-9, Paul repeats a number of these ideas. The faithfulness of God is a dominant theme in this thanksgiving. God has seen to it that the Corinthians are lacking in no good gift. They are rich in speech and knowledge. God will sustain them to the end, guiltless on the day of the Lord.

Later in the same epistle, when Paul portrays himself as a master builder who laid a foundation, Jesus Christ, it is said that everyone must take care to build on that foundation correctly. How each one builds on it will be revealed because the day (of the Lord) will disclose it. Fire will test what sort of work each one has done, and accordingly there will be either reward or punishment. But punishment does not mean someone will not be saved (1 Cor 3:10-15). Paul in this passage may very well be thinking of a reward in this world.[13]

Again, in Rom 13:11-14, we ostensibly find a reflection on the Parousia, or day of the Lord. The Roman Christians should be aware that now is the time to be awake, for their salvation is nearer than before. The day is at hand; they should put on the armor of light and cast off the works of darkness. They are to conduct themselves seemingly as in the day; this means that they leave no room for the flesh and its desires, for reveling and drunkenness, for debauchery and licentiousness, for quarreling and jealousy. Other than the short vice list, the directives in this passage are general and somewhat vague. However, there is no lack of clarity about the demand for moral activity in preparation for the coming salvation.

Twice in the thanksgiving of his Letter to the Philippians Paul has joined moral activity to the day of Jesus Christ. Paul is sure that God, who brought the Philippians into partnership with him for the gospel, will bring that good work to completion on the day of the Lord. He prays that the Philippians' love may abound more and more, with knowledge and all discernment, so that they may approve what is excellent and be pure and blameless for the day of Christ, filled with the fruits of righteousness (Phil 1:5-6,9-11). These words surely remind us of what we have already detected in 1 Thessalonians and 1 Corinthians. Paul, in Phil 2:14-16, wants to be proud on the day of the Lord because he will not have labored among the Philippians in vain. The reason he gives for this pride is the

---

[13]See Roger Mohrlang, *Matthew and Paul: A Comparison of Ethical Perspectives* (Cambridge: University Press, 1984) 61-63. However, this is unusual in Paul and cannot be a means of solving the tension between justification by faith and judgment by works.

moral lives of the Philippians. They will have done everything without grumbling or questioning, will have been blameless and innocent, children of God without blemish in the midst of a crooked and perverse generation among whom they have shone as lights in the world.

The final judgment, too, functions for Paul as a stimulus for moral living. The reader discovers Paul's general understanding on this topic in Rom 14. The Roman Christians are not to pass judgment on one another, for everyone will stand before the judgment seat of God and will give an account (cf. 2 Cor 5:9-10). So, presently one should be fully convinced in his or her own mind as to what to do and then do it for the Lord; no one should act out of doubt. The real task is not to put a stumbling block in anyone's way, but to walk in love, righteousness, peace, joy and mutual up-building.

Whether Paul is addressing the question of the Galatians' participation in the collection for the poor in Jerusalem in Gal 6:7-10 or not,[14] these verses do relate to eschatology and the final judgment, and to a more general statement of the requirement of moral living. The proverbs, "God is not mocked" and "Whatever one sows, that one will also reap," set the tone of the pericope. One's life moves toward either corruption or eternal life. The Galatians should not grow weary or lose heart, but while there is still the opportunity, they should do good to everyone, especially to their fellow Christians.

Certainly, Rom 2:1-16 deals with the final judgment and the necessity of moral living on the part of human beings. The whole passage should probably be understood in the light of v 16, ". . . on that day when, according to my gospel, God judges the secrets of everyone by Christ Jesus." Here, it suffices for our purposes simply to call attention to the fact that at the final judgment individuals will have to account for their actions. Another passage which unites moral activity with the final judgment is Rom 3:3-8. True, the main scope of this passage is Paul's desire to answer those who slanderously

---

[14]John Bligh, *Galatians: A Discussion of St. Paul's Epistle* (Householder Commentaries 1; Lenden: St. Paul Publications, 1969) 483-8.

charge him with saying that one may do evil so that good may come. Yet, Paul states that the Roman Christians should hold on to the truth that God is faithful and will judge the world. Consequently, the final judgment encourages us to act morally because we will have to give an account of what we have done in this world.

Community and Morality

The relationship between the Christian community, whether local or universal, and morality must include what has already been said about our unity with Christ and our being the body of Christ. The Christian community is to preserve moral living. For instance, a man in the Corinthian community was apparently living in an intimate union with his step-mother. The Christians there are not only not upset about the situation; they are boasting about it. Seemingly, Paul's earlier preaching on Christian freedom had been misunderstood. But Paul is very clear on what the Corinthians' present action should be. They are to gather as a community in the name of the Lord Jesus and, with Paul's being among them in spirit, they are to deliver this man to Satan for the destruction of the flesh, that his spirit may be saved on the day of the Lord. Paul is calling for a kind of community excommunication. The explanation offered for this "excommunication" pertains to community: a little yeast has its effect all through the dough, and since Christ, our paschal lamb, has been sacrificed, we should not celebrate the festival with the old leaven of malice and evil, but with the unleavened bread of sincerity and truth. Surely, Paul gives the directive that the man is to be thrown out of the community, but this is to be done by an action of the community and is justified by the evil effect this man's behavior has on the whole community (1 Cor 5:1-8).

The passage continues with the information that Paul had written a previous letter to the Corinthians in which he had instructed them not to associate with immoral individuals. This Pauline directive was to be reinforced by the community's treatment of those who, guilty of immorality, greed, idolatry, reviling, drunkenness or robbery, qualified as immoral. The Corinthians were not even to eat with such an individual, yet the man who is living with his step-mother had not been isolated at all. On the other hand, Paul leaves the judgment of those outside the community to God. It is those inside the Church whom Paul claims the Corinthians are to judge (1 Cor 5:9-13).

Later Paul tells the Romans to take note of those Christians who cause dissensions and difficulties in opposition to the doctrine they have been taught These individuals are to be avoided because they do not serve the Lord Jesus, but their own appetites. They deceive the simple-minded with their flattering words. Unlike them, the true Christians should be wise as to what is good and guileless as to what is evil. Then the God of peace will soon crush Satan under their feet (Rom 16:17-20). The Christian troublemakers in Rome, like those in Corinth, are to be avoided.

A Christian community can also be asked to receive an offender back into its midst. We are ignorant of the identity of the man spoken of in 2 Cor 2:5-11. Very likely, the "Letter of Tears" was written because of the disturbance he had caused, for according to the first verse of this pericope, he had also somehow offended Paul. But now Paul uses the full force of his personality to get the Corinthians to accept him back into the community. Paul contends that the man has suffered enough from his expulsion, and urges the Corinthians to forgive and comfort him lest he be overwhelmed by excessive sorrow. They are to affirm their love for him and to show Paul that they are obedient in everything. Thus, they will keep Satan from gaining the advantage over all of them. If one keeps in mind that Paul was doubtless instrumental in this man's expulsion from the Corinthian community, it is easy to appreciate his love and concern for the offender. Consequently, a community must be disposed to forgive, comfort and manifest their love toward anyone who has gone astray. If he or she repents, one should be accepted back into the community; otherwise, the advantage passes over to Satan.

The *Sitz im Leben* of Paul's Letter to the Philippians may well be that it is an attempt to settle a disagreement between two prominent women in the community. Paul does appeal to Euodia and Syntyche to "think the same thing in the Lord" (Phil 4:2), and this theme of "thinking the same thing (in the Lord)" appears elsewhere in the epistle (2:2,5;3:15). In fact, this idea is at the heart of Phil 2:1-5:

> So if there is any encouragement in Christ, any incentive of love, any participation in the Spirit, any affection and sympathy, complete my joy by being of the same mind, having the same love, being in full accord and of one mind. Do nothing from selfishness or conceit, but in humility count others better than yourselves. Let each of you look not only to his or her own interests, but also to the interests of others. Have this mind among yourselves, which is yours in Christ Jesus.

The theme of "fellowship" likewise plays a significant part in the epistle (1:5,7;2:1;3:10;4:14-15), and Paul's use of "all" (e.g. 1:1,4,7,8,25) brings out his concern for community.[15] What interests us is the moral directive to the members of the community to think the same thing and the approval given to the various expressions of fellowship noted in the epistle.

Visits and Hospitality

Visits promote Christian unity and moral living. Paul very much wants to see the Thessalonians again and to supply what is lacking in their faith. Timothy has returned from them and given Paul the comforting good news of their faith, love and fond memories and of their own desire to see him (1 Thess 2:17-20;3:6-10). Likewise, Timothy will visit the Corinthians and remind them of Paul's ways in the Lord (1 Cor 4:17). When Paul visits them again, he will give directives about their other concerns (1 Cor 11:34). For his part, he does not want to

---

[15]Mary Ann Getty (*Philippians and Philemon,* New Testament Message 14; Wilmington, Delaware: Michael Glazier, 1980, 5) points to some of this evidence.

find them puffed up, but it is up to them to determine whether he is to come with power and the rod, or with love and gentleness (1 Cor 4:18-21). He does not want just to see them in passing, but on his way from Macedonia he hopes to spend some time with them. Paul has also urged Apollos to visit them (1 Cor 16:5-7,12). After his discouraging second visit, Paul still wants to see the Corinthians; however, he does not want another painful visit, but one that would be a double pleasure for them (2 Cor 1:15-17,23-2:3). Paul is fearful of this third visit. They might not find one another as they wish, and Paul himself does not want to have to be severe in the use of his authority. Nonetheless, the Corinthians who sinned before may still be unrepentant; if so, he will not spare them, and they will have the desired proof that Christ is speaking in him with the power of God (2 Cor 12:20-13:4,10).

Paul longs to see the Christians in Rome that they might be mutually encouraged by each others' faith. He wants to impart some spiritual gift to strengthen them and to reap some harvest among them as among the rest of the Gentiles. He is eager to preach the gospel to them (Rom 1:10-15). He will come with the fullness of the blessing of Christ and enjoy their company a bit before he moves on to Spain. Should by God's will all go well as regards the collection in Jerusalem, he will come to them with joy and be refreshed in their company (Rom 15:22-24,29,32). To the Philippians Paul writes that the manner of their life should be worthy of the gospel so that whether he comes and sees them or is absent, he may hear that they stand firm in one spirit and strive for the faith of the gospel, not at all frightened by opponents (Phil 1:27f). He hopes to send Timothy to them to be cheered by news of them. Timothy is genuinely concerned about the Philippians' welfare, and as soon as Paul sees how things fare for himself, he will send him. In fact, Paul trusts that he himself will be able to visit them (Phil 2:19-24). On the other hand, Epaphroditus' visit almost cost him his life, but he brought the Philippians' gifts and completed their service to Paul (cf. Phil 2:25-30;4:18).

Paul instructs the Roman Christians to practice hospitality (Rom 12:13). When Timothy comes, the Corinthians are to put him at ease. No one is to despise him; they should speed

him on his way in peace (1 Cor 16:10f). Later, Titus arrives at
Corinth to bring about their reconciliation with Paul, and they
receive Titus with fear and trembling (2 Cor 7:6-7,13-16).
Apparently, some physical ailment plagued Paul when he first
preached to the Galatians, yet they did not scorn or despise
him, but they received him as an angel of God and would have
plucked out their very eyes and given them to him (Gal
4:12-15).

Not all scholars are convinced that ch. 16 was originally
part of Paul's Letter to the Romans. No matter, Paul commends to its recipients the deaconess Phoebe who they are to
receive in the Lord. She is to get whatever help she needs, for
she has helped many, including Paul himself (vv 1-2). Moreover, Gaius is described in that chapter as host to Paul and to
the whole church (v 23). Finally, Paul asks Philemon to
prepare a guest room for him (Phlm 22). His probable presence
cannot but add more weight to his pleas on Onesimus' behalf.
Consequently, visits and hospitality are aspects of Christian
living. They can demonstrate Christians' love, support and
encouragement of one another. In a sense, visits are encounters,
and one can be called to repentance or challenged to greater
excellence. Visits are opportunities to serve, enjoy one another's
company and be sped upon one's way for the gospel.

Interaction with the Weak in Community

Although the question about weak members has in part
arisen elsewhere in this book, an overall summary of the topic
seems appropriate. "Weakness" is used here in many senses,
and unless otherwise indicated, the present consideration is
based on 1 Cor 8:1-13;10:23-33; Rom 14:1-15:7. The strong
Roman Christians ought to bear with the failings of the weak,
as the Galatians are to restore in a spirit of gentleness anyone
who errs and to look to themselves lest they be tempted (Gal
6:1). No one should be despised or judged because he or she
eats or does not eat some given food, for God is the one who
passes judgment. Nonetheless, Christian liberty is to be subordinated to other values. For instance, those who are weak in

the faith should be welcome, but not for disputes. Nor should the strong Christians become a stumbling block to the weak. So, if a certain kind of food would lead a brother or sister to sin, Paul would never eat it. Christians are to walk in love and not sin against the weak conscience of their brother or sister. Otherwise, they sin against Christ who died for the weak (cf. Rom 5:6-10). Christians are to build up one another. Christ did not please himself, and we are not to seek our own good but that of the neighbor. Like the Roman Christians we ought to do what makes for peace and to live in harmony with one another to the glory of God.

The truth is that the weakness of God is stronger than anything human and that God chose those who were weak and powerless by worldly standards to confound the wise (1 Cor 1:25-27). He gives greater honor to the inferior part of the body that there may be no discord and that the members have the same care for one another. The weaker parts of the body are indispensable, and so we invest them with greater honor and modesty (1 Cor 12:22-26). Paul's own ministerial attitude is to become weak to the weak that he might win the weak for salvation (1 Cor 9:22). His appeal to the Thessalonians is surely practical, "admonish the idlers, encourage the fainthearted, help the weak, be patient with them all" (1 Thess 5:14).

Conclusion

In summary, the salvation which God brings us in Christ bears on our moral living. We are to appreciate and live out the significance of our unity with Christ and of our righteousness, and the "gospel" and knowledge (and equivalent expressions), the resurrection, Parousia and judgment, all elicit moral activity. The assumption is that God's actions constitute the basis for moral living. Our loyalty and worship is to the Father and Jesus, not to idols; we are alive to God in Christ Jesus. We cannot drink the cup of the Lord and the cup of idols.

The evidence we have studied often shows that Paul vaguely

states the nature of the moral activity. Love is mentioned more than any other action, although the doing of good, peace and joy, and service are not far behind. We so live that we preserve our unity with Christ. The gifts of each Christian are to be used for the common good. This unity with Christ provides us with a new self-image, and so we perform good deeds. It does not make us complacent or proud, but generous and much more able to deal with the ups and downs, the suffering in our lives. We reject the flesh and its desires.

The Philippians' partnership in the gospel can be ours. We must lead lives worthy of the gospel message and act out of faith. Grace leads to moral living, generosity and thanksgiving. We are not yet perfect, but we avoid jealousy and strife, grumbling and questioning. We encourage and build up one another and truly discern what God wants so that we can be holy and blameless on the day of the Lord. Hope and not losing heart are characteristic of our lives, and freedom is the opportunity to serve God and one another in love.

The Christian community is to preserve moral living. It may have to expel a member temporarily or not to associate with him or her. However, the scope is positive, a change of heart and acceptance back into the community. Community members should try to think the same thing in the Lord, look to the interests of others and promote harmony. Paul's touching attitude toward the Jewish people becomes an example for us.

Visits promote Christian unity and often constitute a call to moral living. Both visits and hospitality can be occasions of mutual love, support and encouragement. In the community "strong" Christians are to bear with the "weak." Everyone should act out of a good conscience and be spared judgment. Rather everything is to be done to build up the neighbor. Like Christ we are not to please ourselves, and inferior members are an indispensable part of the body and should receive greater honor. In short, we are to live in harmony to the glory of God.

Part II

Paul's Moral Directives to Communities and Individuals

Of course, the designation of this section is somewhat arbitrary since the topic of this whole book could be stated as is the above heading. Nevertheless, some organization is necessary, and the phrasing of this heading does allow us to focus on certain data. "Encourage," "urge" or "appeal" (*parakalēo*) is one way that Paul expresses moral directives (e.g. 1 Thess 2:3; 2 Cor 10:1f;12:18;13:11).[16] Naturally, God and the OT are sources of encouragement (Rom 15:4f). To be sure, encouragement is a gift some Christians have (Rom 12:8). Only two instances of this gift of encouragement are not treated elsewhere. They both appear in Paul's First Letter to the Thessalonians. Timothy is sent by Paul to encourage the Thessalonians lest they be moved by their afflictions (1 Thess 3:2f), and the Thessalonians themselves are to encourage and build up one another, just as they are doing (1 Thess 5:11).

Paul does give his communities any number of moral directives. Frequently, these directives are of a general nature, and some of them we have already studied under other headings.

---

[16]For other Pauline expressions for moral directives see J-F. Collange, *De Jésus à Paul: l'éthique au Nouveau Testament* (Geneva: Labor et Fides, 1980) 20. He notes the following: "encourage" (*paramytheîsthai*), "warn" (*noutheleîn*), "beg" (*deîsthai*), "ask" (*erōtān*), "attest" (*martyreîsthai*), "think" (*nomizein*), "say" (*legein*) and "give one's opinion" (*gnōmēn didonai*). Also, he calls attention to "wish" (*thelein*). S. Zedda (*Relativo e assoluto*, 45) adds "command" (*parangellein*).

3

Further Moral Directives

In his First Letter to the Corinthians, Paul gives further general moral directives. The Corinthians are to so run in the race that they may win the prize. After all, unlike the ordinary athlete, they are after an imperishable crown (1 Cor 9:24-25). In the midst of his presentation on the resurrection, Paul observes, "Do not be deceived: 'Bad company ruins good morals.' Come to your right mind, and sin no more. For some have no knowledge of God. I say this to your shame" (1 Cor 15:33-34). At the very end of that same chapter Paul writes that the Corinthians ought to be steadfast, immovable, always abounding in the work of the Lord, knowing that their labor in the Lord is not in vain (v 58). Lastly, in a final request to the Corinthians, Paul calls them to be watchful, to stand firm in their faith, to be courageous and strong. They ought to do everything in love (1 Cor 16:13).

Paul appeals to the Roman Christians to present their bodies as a living sacrifice, holy and acceptable to God. This is their spiritual worship. They are not to be conformed to this world but to be transformed by the renewal of their mind in order that they might test to see what is the will of God, what is good, acceptable and perfect (Rom 12:1-2).

Christians should be living sacrifices and a spiritual worship. They should know God's will and be of right mind. They are to do everything out of love, to abound in works of the Lord and not to associate with bad companions. Firm in the faith, they are courageous and strong, steadfast and immovable. Their labor is not in vain; their prize is an imperishable crown.

"Indicative" and "Imperative" in Paul's Letters

Often one hears reference to the "indicative" or the "imperative" of a Pauline letter. The "indicative" designates the part of
the letter whose content is Paul's teaching or theology; the
"imperative," on the other hand, marks that part of the letter
where Paul calls for moral action. This distinction between
"indicative" and "imperative" is not to be understood rigidly.
Indicative and imperative material is intertwined throughout
the letters. Nonetheless, there can be little doubt that Paul
does have sections in his letters which are primarily imperative.
To discover this, one need only begin reading the letters at the
following points: 1 Thess 4:1; 1 Cor 12:1; Rom 12:1; Gal 5:13;
Phil 3:17; Phlm 8.[17] These imperative sections demonstrate
Paul's serious attitude toward moral behavior. In this section
only those topics will be treated which are not covered elsewhere in this book.

A number of Paul's directives relate to goodness (*agathos,
kalos* and their cognates). First of all, it is slanderous to charge
Paul with teaching that Christians ought to do evil so that
good may come (Rom 3:8;6:1f). Rather kindness and goodness
are fruits of the Spirit (Gal 5:22). Of course, we do no good on
our own; we depend on God to be able to act thus through
Jesus (Rom 7:18-20,24-25). Kindness is one of the ways in
which Paul commends his ministry (2 Cor 6:6). Paul is sure
that God who began a good work in the Philippians will bring
it to completion at the day of Jesus Christ (Phil 1:6). Doing
good seems to be a description of Christian living; Paul tells
the Galatians, "You were running well" (5:7). Certainly, good
is a criterion for Christian living. The Thessalonians and
Romans are urged to test everything, hold fast to what is
good, and abstain from every form of evil (1 Thess 5:21-22;
Rom 12:2,9). The Romans are to be wise as to what is good
and guileless, as to what is evil (Rom 16:19; cf. Phlm 6).
Christians are not to repay evil for evil, but always to seek to

---

[17]I am well aware of the disputes over the imperative sections themselves and where
they begin. My only point is that these texts do support the existence of imperative
sections in Paul's epistles.

do good to one another and to all (1 Thess 5:15; Rom 12:17), to overcome evil with good (Rom 12:21). They should not let their good be spoken of as evil (Rom 14:6), and everyone should please the neighbor for good, to edify him or her (Rom 15:2; cf. 1 Cor 14:17). The Galatians should not grow weary in doing good, but do good to everyone, especially to those who are of the household of faith (Gal 6:9-10). In 2 Cor 13:5-10, the question of the Corinthians' testing themselves arises. Paul prays that the Corinthians may do no wrong—that they do good even though Paul and the others may seem to have failed. Earlier in the same letter, Paul assures the Corinthians that God is able to provide them with every blessing in abundance; that they may always have enough of everything, and may provide in abundance for every good work (9:8). By way of summary, it can be said that for those who love God everything works toward the good (Rom 8:28).

Good should be done freely. Paul prefers to do nothing without Philemon's consent, in order that his goodness might not be by compulsion but of his own free will (v 14). Moreover, it is always good to be made much of, but this must be done for a good purpose (Gal 4:17-18).

Paul has predicated "good" of several actions. The collection for the poor in Jerusalem is motivated by what is good in the sight of the Lord, and of everyone (2 Cor 8:20-21). Likewise, it is good of the Philippians to share, by their support, in Paul's troubles (Phil 4:14). As a general norm, it is good for the Corinthian men not to touch a woman, if they can successfully live such a lifestyle (1 Cor 7:1). There is no need to fear civil rulers; the Roman Christians are just to do good, and they will win approval (Rom 13:3). Finally, whoever does good will be rewarded (2 Cor 5:10; Gal 6:9; Rom 2:6-11).

Walking as a Moral Directive

The verb "to walk" serves Paul as a means of instructing his communities about Christian living. Of course, this use of "to walk" to describe moral living is Jewish. Paul exhorts the Thessalonians to follow what he has taught them and so "to

walk" and please God. They already walk in this way; he just
wants them to do so more and more. His further exhortations
have the purpose of getting the Thessalonians to walk in an
appropriate manner toward outsiders, and to have need of no
one (1 Thess 4:1,12; cf. 2:11-12).

Paul asks the Corinthians whether they are not fleshly and
walking by a human standard when there is jealousy and strife
among them (1 Cor 3:3). His general norm is that each one
ought to walk as God has called him or her (1 Cor 7:17).
Apparently speaking in the name of Christians, Paul asserts,
"For we walk by faith, not by sight" (2 Cor 5:7). When Paul
speaks of his third visit to them and his love for them, he
wonders about the charge that he took advantage of them. He
asks them, "Did I take advantage of you through any of those
whom I sent to you?. . . . Did Titus take advantage of you?
Did we not walk in the same spirit? Did we not take the same
steps?" (2 Cor 12:17-18). As stated earlier in the letter, Paul has
not walked cunningly (4:2), nor in a worldly fashion (10:23).
He himself is an example to the Corinthians of how to walk.

Paul instructs the Galatians to walk by the Spirit and not to
gratify the desires of the flesh (Gal 5:16). They are to live in
recognition of the new creation which God has achieved in
Christ. If they do, Paul proclaims, "Peace and mercy be upon
all who walk by this rule, upon the Israel of God" (Gal 6:16).

"Walking" is again used as an exhortation for moral living
in Paul's Letter to the Romans. When he speaks of the Christian's dying and rising with Christ in baptism, he contends,
"We were buried therefore with him by baptism into death, so
that as Christ was raised from the dead by the glory of the
Father, we too might walk in newness of life" (Rom 6:4).
Consequently, we are not surprised to read the later exhortation, "Let us walk becomingly as in the day, not in reveling
and drunkenness, not in debauchery and licentiousness, not in
quarreling and jealousy. But put on the Lord Jesus Christ, and
make no provisions for the flesh to gratify its desires" (Rom
13:13-14). A possible description of Christians seems to be:
(those) "who walk not according to the flesh but according to
the Spirit" (Rom 8:4). Finally, if a brother or sister is being
injured by what a Roman Christian is eating, the latter is not
walking in love (Rom 14:15).

The Letter to the Philippians, too, contains a moral exhortation with the image of walking. Paul directs the Philippians to mark those who walk according to his example, for sadly there are many who walk as enemies of the cross of Christ (Phil 3:17f). Consequently, walking for Paul is a way of speaking of Christian living. Often translators render "walk" by "live." Christians walk by faith, light, newness of life and the Spirit and avoid fleshly desires, such as jealousy and strife, drunkenness and licentiousness. Those who so walk in love will receive God's peace and mercy.

4

Paul's Social Teaching

It is not easy to evaluate fairly Paul's social teaching.[18] The reasons for this are threefold. Paul gave a radical significance to the unity of the Christian with Christ. Every other human social relationship was viewed as of relatively little importance in comparison with this basic relationship. This explains why Paul does not think his following statement strange: "So brothers and sisters, in whatever state each was called, there let him or her remain with God" (1 Cor 7:24; cf. 7:17-24). Secondly, Paul and his communities expected that the second coming of Jesus, the Parousia, would be in the very near future. Such an expectation, however, considerably reduces any concentration on questions of social justice; there simply is not much time for change. Finally, there are indications that Paul was concerned about what we would call "the public image" that Christianity gave of itself. He was convinced that Christians ought to put nothing in the way of their ministry (2 Cor 6:3; cf. 1 Cor 9:12b). Some social changes would have been counterproductive because Christianity would have been seen as destructive of accepted social structures and so lose its missionary appeal. Probably the most reasonable evaluation of Paul's teachings on social justice is that, judged by the

---

[18]Wayne A. Meeks (*The First Urban Christians: The Social World of the Apostle Paul*, New Haven: Yale University, 1983) gives a good idea of the context in which many of the following topics are to be situated.

standards of his own time, not ours, he was far ahead of his contemporaries.

Let us review briefly the positions which Paul takes on social issues. He always called for harmony in his communities. This harmony was to manifest itself at the liturgical gatherings (1 Cor 14) and, especially, at the celebrating of the Lord's Supper (1 Cor 11:17-34). Christians were to eat together; there was to be no separation based on circumcision (Gal 2:11-14). The stronger were to build up and not scandalize the weak. No one should judge or look down on a brother or sister. Everyone was to walk in love (1 Cor 8:7-13; Rom 14). The collection for the poor in Jerusalem reveals that any Christian who had more than enough of something should be disposed to share it with those in need (Gal 2:10; cf. 1 Cor 16:1-4; 2 Cor 8-9; Rom 15:25-32). Christians are to practice hospitality (e.g. Rom 12:13; cf. 1 Cor 16:5-7,10-11; 2 Cor 7:13b-16; Rom 16:23; Phlm 22).

Paul even addresses the question of clothing. The notorious passage about the veil on women's heads (1 Cor 11:2-16) has led to any number of studies. In this passage, Paul actually appeals to both men and women. Apparently, he felt that some of the changes in dress at Corinth were contrary to the spirit of the gospel and counterproductive. Paul himself is not totally comfortable with what he has to say, as 1 Cor 11:11-12 demonstrates: "Nevertheless, in the Lord woman is not independent of man nor man of woman; for as woman was made from man, so man is now born of woman. And all things are from God." Nonetheless, he finds some cultural changes unacceptable and so opposes them.[19] Much the same has to be said about 1 Cor 14:33b-36. True, in this context Paul is demanding orderly conduct from everyone, but if 1 Cor 14:33b-36 is not a

[19]The exact nature of Paul's difficulty with how some of the Christians were dressing is not easy to determine. However, I do not think that J. P. Meier, "On the Veiling of Hermeneutics (1 Cor 11:2-16)," *CBA* 40 (1978) 212-26 nor J. Murphy-O'Connor, "Sex and Logic in 1 Corinthians 11:2-16," *CBA* 42 (1980) 482-500 are correct in their respective interpretations of the passage. See J. J. Kilgallen (*First Corinthians: An Introduction and Study Guide*, New York: Paulist, 1987, 94-9) for a good concise explanation.

later insertion, its explanation depends on social customs of the time: women did not generally speak in public and, since they had little, if any, opportunity for education, they would not always understand what was being said. In fairness to Paul, it should not be forgotten that he did give equal rights to both husband and wife, as the parallel structure of the passage on marriage testifies (1 Cor 7:1-5,10-16).[20]

Another social phenomenon which annoys Paul is the practice in Corinth of going to court against a fellow Christian, and this before unbelievers (1 Cor 6:1-8). Such problems ought to be solved by the Christians themselves, some of whom must be wise enough to settle such matters. Rather than have such lawsuits, they should be willing to suffer wrong and be defrauded; but instead, they wrong and defraud. Their behavior is not worthy of the name, "Christian."

Socially, Christians should support one another. As noted above, there was the collection for the poor in Jerusalem. In addition, Paul is grateful for the financial support that the Philippians gave him personally (e.g. Phil 4:10-20; cf. 2 Cor 11:7-11). As a prisoner, Paul was again assisted by the Philippians (Phil 2:25-30), and he implies that Philemon would have been willing to do the same (Phlm 13-14). On another point, the first impression gathered from Paul's letters is that he thought slaves should remain slaves (1 Cor 7:21-24) and, given his deep conviction about a Christian's unity with Christ and the imminent final coming, this impression is true. However, Paul's Letter to Philemon nuances this conclusion a bit. Paul does not direct Philemon to free Onesimus,[21] but there is the vague and suggestive comment, "Confident of your obedience,

[20]See under the next heading, "Marriage and Celibacy." Confer also F. X. Cleary, "Women in the New Testament: St. Paul and the Early Pauline Churches," *BTB* 10 (1980) 78-82. P. Perkins (*Ministering in the Pauline Churches* [New York: Paulist, 1982] 41-3,49-71,92-110) provides an informative and balanced presentation of the topic, as does J. J. Kilgallen, *First Corinthians*, 63-76. O. L. Yarbrough (*Not like the Gentiles: Marriage Rules in the Letters of Paul*, ed. C. H. Talbert; SBLDS 80; Atlanta: Scholars, 1985, 89-125) has a good overall presentation of 1 Cor 7.

[21]The data in the letter simply does not justify such a conclusion, despite the contention of Mary Ann Getty *Philippians and Philemon*, 78-80. Compare S. Lyonnet, *La vie selon L'Esprit*, 252f.

I write to you, knowing that you will do even more than I say" (Phlm 21).

According to Paul, Christians are to respect those in authority. He himself should have been commended by the Corinthians, and not forced to play the fool (2 Cor 12:11-13). Paul instructs the Thessalonians, "But we beseech you, brothers and sisters, to respect those who labor among you and are over you in the Lord and admonish you, and to esteem them very highly in love because of their work" (1 Thess 5:12-13; cf. 1 Cor 16:15-18; Rom 16:3-5). Christians are also to respect civil leaders (Rom 13:1-7). After all, they get their power from God. If one does good, he or she has no need to fear; in fact, civil leaders will praise and protect you from evil. Hence, the Christian's conscience requires observance of civil laws, appropriate respect and the paying of taxes.

Finally, in one of his letters to the Corinthians Paul wrote that they were not to associate with immoral individuals (1 Cor 5:9-11; cf. 15:33).

Marriage and Celibacy

Paul expands on some of his moral directives. This is the case for Christian marriage and celibacy. The Pauline considerations on marriage are to be found in 1 Cor 7:1-40; 9:5; and 2 Cor 6:14-7:1; 11:2-3. It is important to note that Paul's scope in 1 Cor 7:1-40 was not to provide the Corinthians with the ideal description of Christian marriage. Rather, he addresses a question that the Corinthians raised, "Is it well for a man not to touch a woman," and the problem that some of the men are frequenting temple prostitutes; because of the temptation to immorality, Paul advises that each man should have his own wife and each woman her own husband. The parallel structure of 1 Cor 7:2-5, 10-16 leaves no doubt that Paul holds that the husband and wife are equal partners. Each is entitled to conjugal rights, neither rules over his or her own body, and neither can refuse the other, except by mutual agreement. If a separation occurs, neither is to remarry, and either one of them can sanctify the spouse and children or be guiltless, should the non-believing partner depart. A true appreciation of Paul's amazingly progressive stance that "...likewise the husband does not rule over his own body, but the wife does," can only be gained by reading a passage like Sir 42:9-14. Perhaps, two hundred years separate the two passages, but Paul's is light years beyond Sirach and remarkably freeing for the wife.

Jesus' command against divorce is known to Paul and, of course, he quotes it with approval. However, he adds a special condition for someone who was in a pagan marriage and has converted to Christianity (1 Cor 7:12-16). The converted Christian is not to leave the pagan partner if he or she is willing to live together, for the unbelieving partner is sanctified (*hagiazein*) by the believer; otherwise, the children would be unclean, but as it is they are holy. If the unbelieving partner desires to separate, fine; the Christian is not bound. The pericope closes with the puzzling statement, "Wife, how do you know whether you will save your husband? Husband, how do you know whether you will save your wife?" The determining factor in the decision stated above is the pagan partner's attitude toward the faith of the Christian. It seems that the pagan partner's willingness to live together is sufficient to bind the Christian to the marriage and to enable him or her to become the means of sanctification for the whole family. Paul normally uses "made holy" or sanctification of someone who is a Christian, and he claims a valid application of this concept to the pagan spouse and children of such a marriage. So, the Christianity of the believing partner can "christianize" the whole family, and faith has become a significant element of marriage.

If the pagan partner separates (vv 15-16), there is no reason to conclude that Paul is thinking of a real divorce. In fact, the context of a general call to celibacy argues against such a conclusion. Nor is it correct to conclude from this passage that Paul was in favor of marriages to pagans. He was not, as 1 Cor 7:39 testifies: "If the husband dies, she (the wife) is free to be married to whom she wishes, *only in the Lord*" (Interestingly, Paul recognizes the woman's right to pick her partner.) Although 2 Cor 6:14-7:1 may well be an insertion, Paul may have made it himself, for he would not find the imperative, "Do not be mismated with unbelievers," inconsistent with his own thought.

Paul believes that marrying is a good thing to do, but celibacy is better (1 Cor 7:38). There are a number of reasons why he adopted this position. His thought is strongly influenced by the conviction that Jesus will soon come again. Moreover, Paul himself found celibacy a very effective way of serving the Lord. He was aware of his right to marry (1 Cor 9:5). Perhaps he was a widower, but that is a conjecture without any strong support. Anyway, he chose celibacy. Paul is aware of different gifts (1 Cor 7:7), and among other indications his use of marriage as a description of how he has betrothed the Corinthians to Christ reveals his recognition of its dignity (2 Cor 11:2-3). Nevertheless, so personally beneficial was his own experience of celibacy that he advises the Corinthians who can to remain celibate as he is (1 Cor 7:6-9, 25-28,32-38). According to Paul, the celibate is free of worldly anxieties and can concentrate on the affairs of the Lord, and on how to please him. (Probably we have here the strongest argument for holding that Paul was never married, for he has not worked out the spirituality of a married person.) All of this may appear as just so much theoretical reasoning if a reader does not reflect that individuals are not always clear on whether or not God's call is to one state or the other. Moreover, the divorce rate and early death of a marriage partner increase the likelihood of the present day applicability of the passage. Certainly, celibacy allows for an intense concentration on the things of the Lord.

The Lord's Supper

The celebration of the Lord's Supper is surely a social occasion. As a sacred meal, it actualizes the Christians' union with the body of Christ (1 Cor 10:16-17; cf. vv 1-22), and thus they cannot participate in any other sacred meal. Otherwise, they would be idolaters as were some of the Jews in the wilderness. Nor are Christians to imitate their immorality or testing of the Lord, nor their grumbling. Their failings were written as a warning. Yet, God is faithful and will not let the Christians be tested beyond their strength.

Furthermore, Paul left instructions for the celebration of the Lord's Supper (1 Cor 11:17-34). Most importantly, Christians are to continue to celebrate it, as the traditional statement, "Do this in remembrance of me" (v 24; cf. vv 25-26; Luke 22:19b), shows. Wealthier Christians may have provided for these meals. However, in accord with the social customs of the times, a greater quantity and a better quality of food and drink may have been served to their social equals than to participants of lower social status. But, according to Paul, these celebrations should not be marked by divisions. No one should eat ahead of the others or be drunk. No one should be humiliated because he or she has nothing. Instead, they should wait for one another, and those who are hungry should eat at home.

Lastly, the bread and the cup of the Lord must be eaten in a worthy manner. Certainly, this is in part a reference to the conduct spoken of above because vv 33-34 return to that topic. However, it should not be limited to that. Most reasonably, to be "guilty of profaning the body and blood of the Lord" (v 27) is to fail to act in accord with what Paul has just described the Lord's Supper to be. This interpretation is supported by Paul's introduction of v 27 with *Hōste*, "therefore," which points to a conclusion from what was just said. The further description of the offense as "without discerning the body" (v 29) relates more directly to the Lord's Supper than to one's conduct at it. After all, "body" in this context more obviously relates to Jesus' body in the Lord's Supper than to the body of Christ mentioned earlier in the letter. So, Paul is not only concerned with conduct at the meal, but likewise with the faith that leads to such conduct.[22]

[22]For a similar interpretation of this passage, see H. Conzelmann, *1 Corinthians* (Philadelphia, Fortress, 1975) 192-203 and J. J. Kilgallen, First Corinthians, 107f.

The Collection

The collection for the poor in Jerusalem is another social issue on which Paul expands his moral directives. He had been asked by the Church in Jerusalem to make this collection (Gal 2:10), and he was eager to do so since among other things it was an opportunity to encourage Christian unity. As noted earlier, he viewed the collection as God's grace and doing.

Paul praised the liberality of the Macedonians who, though poor, saw the collection as a grace and first gave of themselves, then even beyond their means (2 Cor 8:1-5). With this example, Paul exhorts the Corinthians to complete, and even to excel, with their gracious gift. Their earnestness will demonstrate that their love is genuine. They are not to be burdened while others are eased, but an equality should be established so that their present abundance may supply for the need of those in Jerusalem. In short, they should be like Jesus; although he was rich, he became poor for them (2 Cor 8:6-15,24).

In 2 Cor 9, the Corinthians are told about how Paul has been boasting to the Macedonians about their readiness for the collection. He does not want either the Corinthians or himself to be humiliated in this. Actually, their zeal stirred up the majority of Macedonians. The Corinthians' contribution should not be an exaction but a willing gift. If they sow bountifully, they will reap bountifully. The Lord loves a cheerful giver, and their generosity will bring about thanksgiving to God.

Paul writes the Romans that Macedonia and Achaia were pleased to share with the poor among the saints in Jerusalem. They are in debt to the latter because they share in their spiritual blessings, so they ought to serve them with their material blessings (Rom 15:26-28). Consequently, the collection is God's gift to the Macedonian and Achaian communities. The lowest motivation for their good act is to avoid embarrassment; the highest is to imitate Christ, who became poor that they might be rich. Their liberality and generosity will bring thanks to God.

Death

Of course, there is the general directive of dying and rising with Christ that bears on our lives, both here and to come. However, Paul does give some other directives about Christian death. The Thessalonians should not grieve as others who do not have hope. They should, on the contrary, console one another with the belief that Christ will come again, and that they all will be raised with him (1 Thess 4:13-18; cf. 1 Cor 15:12-25). He tells the Corinthians that we groan and are anxious here, and long to put on our heavenly dwelling. However, we are always of good courage (2 Cor 5:2-6). It is necessary that Christ rule and put all enemies under his feet. The last enemy is death (1 Cor 15:25-26). We will be able to mock death because it is swallowed in the victory which God gives us in our Lord Jesus Christ. Thus, we owe thanks to God and, as Paul concludes, we should be "steadfast, immovable, always abounding in the work of the Lord, knowing that in the Lord your labor is not in vain" (1 Cor 15:58; cf. vv 51-57).

5

Paul's Challenge, "Be Imitators of Me as I Am of Christ"

Another moral directive that Paul gives his communities is that they ought to imitate him (1 Cor 4:16; Phil 3:17; 4:9). At times he expresses it more in accord with his whole theology and says, "imitate me as I imitate Christ" (1 Cor 11:1; cf. 1 Thess 1:6). Let us see if we can determine what Paul is calling his individual communities to imitate.

Suffering as well as joyful reception and proclamation of the word are ways Paul sees the Thessalonians imitating himself and the Lord (1 Thess 1:6-10; cf. 2:14). Later in the epistle there is confirmation that through suffering and proclamation of the word the Thessalonians imitate the Lord and Paul himself. We read in 1 Thess 2:14-16:

> For you, brothers and sisters, became imitators of the churches of God in Christ Jesus which are in Judea; for you suffered the same things from your own people as they did from the Jews, who killed both the Lord Jesus and the prophets, and drove us out, and displease God and oppose everyone by hindering us from speaking to the Gentiles that they may be saved. . . .

In 1 Cor 4 (v 16), Paul urges the Corinthians to, "be imitators of me." This chapter is a unit, and addresses the question of Paul's ministry (cf. 1 Cor 9:1-2,19-23;15:9-11; 2 Cor 4:1-12,16-

18;6:3-10). Hence, it is only logical to conclude that Paul wants the Corinthians to imitate him as he is portrayed in this chapter. Apollos, Cephas and Paul are servants of Christ and stewards of the mysteries of God. A steward must be trustworthy. Although he is not conscious of doing anything wrong, Paul is not concerned about any human judges. He does not even judge himself; he leaves that to Christ. Nor should the Corinthians show favoritism or be puffed up. There follows a contrast between the Corinthians' present view of themselves and the realities of the life of an apostle. The Corinthians are boastful and feel satisfied and rich; they even see themselves as reigning. But the apostles are last of all (cf. 15:8-11), like persons sentenced to death, a spectacle to all. They are fools for Christ's sake, weak, and held in disrepute, whereas the Corinthians are convinced of their own wisdom, strength and honor. The apostles, however, continue to be hungry, thirsty, ill-clad, buffeted and homeless. They work with their own hands, and when reviled, persecuted and slandered, they bless, endure and conciliate. They are the refuse of the world. All of this has been said not to shame the Corinthians, but to admonish them. They have countless guides, but Paul has, through the gospel, become their father. The Corinthians are to note how Paul ministers and imitate him.

Paul again gives attention to imitation of himself and of Christ in 1 Cor 11:1. Toward the end of 1 Cor 10, Paul returns to the question of eating meat offered to idols, and to the respect that a Christian should have for another's conscience and upbuilding. He concludes this chapter with the following general statement, and immediately afterwards repeats the theme of imitation:

> So, whether you eat or drink, or whatever you do, do all to the glory of God. Give no offense to Jews or to Greeks or to the Church of God, *just as I try to please everyone in everything I do,* not seeking my own advantage but that of many, that they may be saved (1 Cor 10:31-33; cf. 9:19-23).

Everything should be done for the glory of God. Like Paul, the Corinthians are not to seek their own advantage and must try to please everyone so that they may be saved.

It is a little more difficult to determine Paul's exact meaning in Gal 4:12 (cf. 4:12-19): "Brothers and sisters, I beseech you, become as I am, for I also have become as you are." A clue to the solution is to consider what comes immediately before and after this verse in the Letter to the Galatians. Immediately before it, Paul fears that he may have labored in vain among the Galatians who are turning back and becoming slaves of the weak and beggarly elemental spirits, beings that are no gods. They are likewise observing days, months, seasons and years. Right after our verse, Paul asks, "Tell me, you who desire to be under the law, do you not hear the law?" (v 21). He then goes on with the allegory of the two women who begot sons to Abraham, the slave and the free woman. Again, Paul is in travail that Christ be formed in the Galatians. Consequently, to be like Paul is to be formed in Christ, to be a Christian; and further, to be in slavery no longer, but to be free.

Paul commands the Philippians, "Brothers and sisters, join in imitating me, and mark those who so live as you have an example in us" (Phil 3:17; cf. 3:12-4:1). In the next verse Paul states whom the Philippians are not to imitate, namely, enemies of the cross of Christ, whose end is destruction, whose god is their belly, who glory in their shame and set their minds on earthly things. The Christians' commonwealth is in heaven, and Jesus Christ will change their lowly bodies to be glorious like his own. Therefore, they are to stand firm in the Lord. Furthermore, in the previous verses (Phil 3:7-16) Paul tells us how he is acting until he attains the resurrection of the dead, and he already brings up the theme of imitation, "Let those of us who are mature be thus minded; and if in anything you are otherwise minded, God will reveal that also to you" (v 15). Paul has subordinated everything else in his life to belief in Christ. He wants to share in Christ's sufferings so that he might attain the resurrection. He is not perfect, but forgets what lies behind and strains toward what lies ahead. So the Philippians' Christian living should be based not on earthly values, but on those determined by Jesus' resurrection. Christ must be the center of their lives, and they should be willing to share in his suffering. In him they stand firm and strive toward the goal of the resurrection.

Later the Philippians are told, "What you have learned and received and heard and seen in me, do; and the God of peace will be with you" (Phil 4:9). Paul is convinced that everything he said or did was worthy of imitation. Moreover, since v 9 is joined grammatically with v 8, we have a further explanation of what things about Paul the Philippians are to imitate. They are to think about whatever is true, honorable, just, pure, lovely, gracious, excellent and worthy of praise. Apparently, they have either heard or seen such in Paul, and are to do likewise themselves.

Paul contends that the Corinthians are not restricted by him, but by their own emotions. Actually, Paul's mouth is open for the Corinthians; his heart is wide; in return, the Corinthians ought to widen their hearts (2 Cor 6:11-13; cf. 7:2).

In summary, Paul has spoken about imitation of himself in all of his genuine letters, except Romans and Philemon. The former had yet to see him, while the theme is only implied in the latter. Most correctly, Paul's challenge was that he should be imitated as he imitated Christ. In fact, Paul centers his life on Christ and subordinates everything else to this basic commitment. He feels that everything that he said and did was worthy of imitation. Particularly, he imitates Christ in his suffering. Moreover, Paul is a servant of Christ and tries to please everyone so as to win them to the gospel. Firm in Christ, he presses toward the goal of his resurrection.

Before leaving the topic of the imitation of Paul, something further needs to be said. Some of Paul's activity may not fit formally under the heading of "imitation" but certainly relates to that topic and could not have been missed by Paul's readers.

To organize the evidence, I will to some extent follow my article, "The Humane Saint Paul.[23]" Here I want only to highlight additional activity of Paul which he doubtless wanted also to be imitated. Four areas are treated: relationship with

---

[23]R. F. O'Toole, "The Humane St. Paul," *Review for Religious* 41 (1982) 80-90. This article offers a fuller treatment than I can present here.

communities, accusations made against him, his weaknesses, and how he dealt with his imprisonment.

Paul dedicated himself to the good of his communities (e.g. 1 Cor 7:35; Phil 2:17-18) and feels very close to them. His images of being their mother (1 Thess 2:7; Gal 4:19) and father (1 Thess 2:11; 1 Cor 4:14-15), and his claim to be their apostle (Gal 1:1,15-16; Rom 1:5-7), and other expressions of close association all speak of the depth of these relationships. Paul tells them he loves them (e.g. 1 Thess 2:8; 1 Cor 16:24; 2 Cor 2:4; Phil 4:1). He delicately phrases every mention of a visit so that the positive aspects outweigh the negative. He never asks for money for himself. If he refuses financial support, this proves his love (2 Cor 11:7-11). He thanks God for what he has done in each community and showers compliments on his communities for their reception of the gospel, their good lives, and as a stimulus to further good acts. Even the greetings in Paul's letters manifest his desire to have a good rapport with and among his communities. Finally, Paul supports other church leaders (1 Cor 3:5-6,22-23; Rom 16:1-7,12-13; Phil 4:2-3) because the same God works in all of them for the growth of the body of Christ, his Son.

Personal accusations can be handled adroitly by Paul. Perhaps 2 Corinthians contains the most such "insults." To our present study, it matters little whether these accusations came from either the "super apostles" or some of the Corinthians. Although there is some discussion, the following are certainly meant as insults: his letters are not easy to understand (1:13), he is fickle (1:17-22), he commends himself (3:1;5:12; cf. 12:1,11), he should have letters of recommendation (3:1-3), he makes a poor appearance and does not speak well (10:1,10-11;11:6), he is an inferior apostle (11:5-6,12-15;12:11-13), he was crafty and got the better of them (12:16), and Christ was not speaking in him (13:3). Paul does not respond to all of these with the same calm tranquility, but he is never vicious, and at times his reactions are a remarkable example for Christians of any age. Let us look at two examples.

When he is accused of being fickle and of saying "Yes" and "No" (1:17-22), Paul does not go into a tirade. After he has implied that he has not been fickle, he turns the charge into a very brief homily about God's fidelity. Paul's word to them has not at the same time been "Yes" and "No." In Jesus, it has always been "Yes"; all the promises of God find their "Yes" in him. A little further on, he most candidly and affectionately states:

> But I call God to witness against me—it was to spare you that I refrained from coming to Corinth.... For I made up my mind not to make you another painful visit. For if I cause you pain, who is there to make me glad but the one whom I have pained.... For I wrote you out of much affliction, and anguish of heart and with many tears, not to cause you pain but to let you know the abundant love that I have for you (1:23-2:4).

Even more touching and loving is his response to the implied or explicit request for letters of recommendation (3:1-3). Paul was the apostle, founder and father of the Corinthian community; the Corinthians were his workmanship in the Lord (1 Cor 3:6-10;4:14-15;9:1-2). This request for letters of recommendation is best understood if one reflects how silly it would be to ask one's mother or father for letters of recommendation as a parent. But, again, Paul is not outraged; with winning and caring charm he just contends that the Corinthians are his letter of recommendation. They are not an ordinary letter, but one written on their hearts and known and read by everyone. They are not written with ink, but with the Spirit of the living God. Surely, such Christian responses to unpleasant and unreasonable accusations were to be imitated by Paul's readers.

Paul actually develops a theology for dealing with his weaknesses. Above, it was observed that Paul was accused of making a poor appearance and of not speaking well (cf. 2 Cor 10:10f; 11:6). He openly admits to this, as well as to some bodily ailment in Galatia which seems to have been some problem with his eyes (Gal 4:13-15). After Paul has reflected on his visions and revelations of the Lord, he relates that to keep him from being too elated by the abundance of revelations he was given a thorn in the flesh, a messenger of Satan, to harass him. Three times he asked God in prayer that it should leave him. The answer he receives is, "My grace is sufficient for you, for my power is made perfect in weakness" (2 Cor 12:9; cf. vv 1-10). Thus, Paul came to his theology of weakness. He could gladly boast about his weaknesses in order that the power of Christ might rest on him. He could be content with weaknesses, insults, hardships, persecutions and calamities; for in these he received the strength of Christ. Actually, Paul's theology of weakness belongs to his main theme of the Christian's unity with Christ, particularly, dying and rising with Christ. The following passage best makes this point:

> . . . Since you desire proof that Christ is speaking in me. He is not weak in dealing with you, but is powerful in you. For he was crucified in weakness, but lives by the power of God. For we are weak in him, but in dealing with you we shall live with him by the power of God (2 Cor 13:3-4; cf. v 9).

No scholar has ever succeeded in determining, to everyone's satisfaction, what Paul meant by the "thorn in the flesh."[24] Perhaps this is best, because we can all identify it with our own weaknesses. We can unite ourselves and our weaknesses with Christ's death so that we experience the power of his resurrection in our lives. Obviously, this theology of weakness can guide us when, like Paul, we are at times discouraged and depressed (2 Cor 1:8-10; 2:12-13; 7:5).

Even in his imprisonment, Paul leaves us an example to imitate. In his genuine letters there are two prison epistles: Philippians and Philemon. A theme of joy dominates Paul's Letter to the Philippians even though he is in prison.[25] His imprisonment is for Christ and for the defense of the gospel (Phil 1:13,16; Phlm 9). It leads the Christians to be more bold and to speak the word of God without fear. Paul rejoices that Christ is proclaimed, whether it be in pretense or truth (Phil 1:12-18). He is grateful to the Philippians for sharing in his

---

[24]S. Lyonnet (*La vie selon L'Esprit*, 263-83) relates the thorn in the flesh to the difficulties that Paul encountered in his apostolate.

[25]Phil 1:4,18,25;2:2,17f,28f;3:1;4:1,4,10.

imprisonment and for sending Epaphroditus to assist him. He is confident that he will remain and continue to work among them (Phil 1:7,24-25; 2:25-30) and that his imprisonment will turn to his own deliverance. Paul hopes that now, as always, Christ will be honored in his body, whether by life or death; for him, to live is Christ, and to die is gain. Presently he shares in Christ's suffering (Phil 1:19-21; 3:10). Though in prison, Paul in his Letter to Philemon is concerned about Onesimus whom he converted, while there. There is little doubt that Paul uses his imprisonment as leverage to argue on Onesimus' behalf (Phlm 9,10,13). So, even in prison, one can be joyful and thoughtful of others. It can be an occasion for further spread of the gospel and deeper union with Christ, and one can particularly share in Christ's suffering. Of course, gratitude is in place for any assistance received.

Consequently, Paul gives any number of moral directives to his communities and to individuals. Certain sections of his letters have even been designated "imperatives." With God's help, Christians are to do the good and walk not according to the flesh but according to the Spirit. Paul's social teachings should be judged in view of his emphasis on unity with Christ, the near expectation of Jesus' return and Paul's conviction that nothing should stand in the way of one's ministry. The latter criterion relates especially to the question of clothing. Paul calls his communities to live in harmony and mutual support. A fellow Christian should not be accused before a pagan judge. On the question of justice for women, Paul was certainly ahead of his time, particularly, as regards marriage; but his personal experience led him to place considerable stress on celibacy. The Lord's Supper actualizes the believer's unity with Christ and should be celebrated accordingly. The collection for the poor in Jerusalem supports unity and was an opportunity for mutual sharing of gifts. Certainly, Christians will all die, but we live in hope and good courage because our labor is not in vain. Finally, we are to imitate Paul as he imitates Christ. We do this especia'y in suffering. We are servants and for the sake of the gospel strive to please everyone. Firm in Christ, we press toward the goal of our resurrection. Likewise worthy of our imitation are Paul's affectionate relations with his various communities, his adroit handling of negative criticism, his theology for dealing with his own weaknesses and his reaction to imprisonment for the gospel.

Part III

The Way to Live Awaiting the Parousia: Gifts and Christian Conduct

In Part I we reviewed the various ways that Christian morality for Paul finds its source in God, Christ and the Spirit, and in what God has done in Christ. Part II considered Paul's moral directives to communities or individuals. This brings us to the question of gifts, and to a further consideration of how Christians should live. Of course, all of these gifts and the whole of Christian living are God's achievement in and for us and others (1 Cor 12:27-31a; Rom 12:3-8). First we will consider Paul's view of the human person, next the gifts about which Paul writes; then we will address virtue and vice catalogs.

6

Paul's View of the Human Person

Paul is not a Greek philosopher, nor has Greek philosophy had any significant influence on his description of human beings. For Paul, human beings who have not embraced God's activity in Christ are under sin and lack the glory of God (Rom 3:9,22-23). For instance, the Galatians are told that formerly they were in bondage to beings that by nature are no gods (4:8). On our own we human beings are simply not capable of doing good, although we do want to do it (Rom 7:9-25). However, one should not conclude from this that Paul held human nature to be evil; the incarnation itself would have kept him from drawing such a conclusion. It is better to say that Paul never really posed the question of what human nature is *in itself*. He always viewed human beings in their relationship with God, and his conclusion was that we are totally dependent on him. We are earthen vessels that the potter, God, makes and uses as he sees fit (cf. 2 Cor 4:7; Rom 9:19-29).

Paul has, however, reflected about human nature in its relationship with God. He speaks of our "flesh" (*sarx*), "body" (*sōma*), "heart" (*kardia*), "soul" (*psychē*), as well as of our "mind" (*nous*) and "spirit" (*pneuma*). Each of these designations refers to the whole human being viewed under a given aspect. "Flesh" generally points to humans in so far as they are inclined away from God and to sin. Perhaps the clearest Pauline treatment of flesh is to be found in Rom 8:3-9. The flesh kept the just requirement of the law from being fulfilled.

Walking according to the flesh is contrasted with walking according to the Spirit. Those who walk according to the flesh move toward death (cf. Gal 5:19-21). Their mind is hostile to God and does not submit to his law; those in the flesh cannot please God.

"Body" can be used in a negative sense, and then it is more or less the equivalent of "flesh." Likewise, "body" can simply specify a person or denote the visible biological aspect of a human being. Of course, our main interest would fix on when "body" is similar to "flesh" and means movement away from God. The contrast between the earthly body and the heavenly, given in 1 Cor 15:42-49, is of secondary interest to us since it does not immediately bear on morality.

Paul does not use "soul" that often. When he does, it usually designates the person of a human being. In addition, it can mean the human mind (Phil 1:27) or point to human life as lived in this world and, thus, be negative by comparison with the "spiritual" (1 Cor 2:14;15:44-46).

Both "heart" and "mind" can signify our human ability to understand and make intellectual judgments. However, "heart" is not always to be understood positively. It can be hardened (2 Cor 3:14), darkened (Rom 1:21; cf. 2 Cor 3:15), doubtful (Rom 10:6-7), lustful (Rom 1:24), and impenitent (Rom 2:5). Only twice does Paul write that the "mind" is capable of misguided activity: he speaks of its baseness (Rom 1:28) and being without fruit (1 Cor 14:14). Paul, in the genuine epistles, uses neither "heart" nor "mind" that often. In the majority of cases, these words look to positive human intellectual activity. For instance, our mind does direct us to follow the law of God (Rom 7:25), and the Gentile could clearly perceive the invisible nature of God through the things that have been made (Rom 1:18-23).

"Spirit" is Paul's most positive description of a human being. It signifies the human person as knowing and willing and being open to the activity of the Holy Spirit. So close is the interaction between our spirit and the Holy Spirit that it is not easy to determine instances where "spirit" definitely refers to the human spirit. However, a number of Paul's one hundred and twenty uses of "spirit" in the genuine epistles do refer to the human spirit.[26] The following citation should suffice to give the reader a feel for Paul's notion of the human spirit: "For what person knows a human being's thoughts except the spirit which is in him or her? So also no one comprehends the thoughts of God except the Spirit of God" (1 Cor 2:11).[27]

Before we conclude this treatment of the human being according to Paul, we ought to view "conscience." "Conscience" for Paul is the intellectual ability to reflect on the truth (ideally, the gospel; cf. 2 Cor 4:2;5:11), and so to come to a judgment as to what is right or wrong, what should be done and what should not. Conscience can witness to a person that he or she has acted honorably (2 Cor 1:12; Rom 2:15-16;9:1). On the other hand, one's conscience can be misguided and lead to an incorrect conclusion about how one is to act morally (1 Cor 8:7;10:28-29; Rom 14:2-6,14,23).[28] Nevertheless, conscience has a supremacy in determining activity because, even if it is erroneous, the person must follow its directive (Rom 13:5;14:5-6,14,23). Should one's conscience be misguided, others whose consciences are directing them correctly are not to look down on such a person but to so live that he or she is not scandalized but "built up." Each one is to seek the good of the neighbor (1 Cor 8:9-13;10:23-30). My conscience may allow me to perform a given act, but if that action would lead my neighbor to sin, I should rather act out of love and build up my neighbor.

Paul's reflections on conscience show a compassionate aware-

---

[26]For example, see 1 Thess 5:23; 1 Cor 2:11;5:3-5;7:34;14:32(?);16:18; 2 Cor 2:13;7:1(?),13; Gal 6:1(?),18; Phil 1:27;4:23; Phlm 25.

[27]Here, I have been following to some extent the lead of J. A. Fitzmyer in *Paul and His Theology: A Brief Sketch* 2nd. Ed. (Englewood Cliffs, NJ: Prentice Hall, 1989) 82-4. See also S. Zedda, *Relativo e assoluto*, 78-81.

[28]J. Murphy-O'Connor ("Freedom or the Ghetto [1 Cor VIII 1-13, X 23-XI 1]," *RB* 85 [1978] 543-74) furnishes a reasonable explanation of the nature of the tensions that Paul deals with in these chapters and his response to them. See also R. Horsley, "Consciousness and Freedom among the Corinthians: 1 Corinthians 8-10," *CBA* 40 (1978) 574-89; R. Schnackenburg, *The Moral Teaching of the New Testament* (Kent: Burns & Oates, 1965) 287-96.

ness of the possibility of consciences reaching different con-
clusions. He does not deny truth or objectivity but calls for
love and the building up of the neighbor. However, he does
not encourage disputes with those who are weak in faith (Rom
14:1).

In summary, Paul's vision of the human being is Jewish.
We depend totally on God for salvation and for good moral
living. On the other hand, the whole human person can be
viewed under different aspects, and each has his or her own
conscience. Openness to the Spirit is imperative, and we should
so live as to build up our neighbor.

7

Gifts and Christian Conduct

Love

For Paul, love is at the center of Christian life and morality.[29] Love is a "still more excellent way" (1 Cor 12:31). It is greater than faith or hope, and the command, "You shall love your neighbor as yourself," fulfills the whole law. It is the one thing Christians owe everyone else, and which does not permit us to do any wrong to a neighbor (1 Cor 13:13; Gal 5:14; Rom 13:8-10). Christians should make love their aim and see to it that everything they do is done in love (1 Cor 14:1;16:14). All of this demonstrates that Paul feels that love serves as a means of discovering exactly what a Christian should do in a given moral situation. Love directs us not to harm the neighbor or ourselves.

Paul has described for his readers the kind of love he has in mind. Let's look at the two main passages which relate these Pauline qualities of love:

> Love is patient and kind; love is not jealous or boastful; it is not arrogant or rude. Love does not insist on its own way; it is not irritable or resentful; it does not rejoice at wrong, but

---

[29]S. Lyonnet *La vie selon L'Esprit,* 223-33; H. Schürmann, "Haben die paulinischen Wertungen," 245-9,252-5,263-5. C. Spicq, *Vie morale et Trinité Sainte,* 58-68 and *Agapé dans le Nouveau Testament* (EBib; Paris: J. Gabalda, 1959) 2:271-305.

rejoices in the right. Love bears all things, believes all things, hopes all things, endures all things. Love never ends; as for prophecies, they will pass away; as for tongues, they will cease; as for knowledge, it will pass away. (1 Cor 13:4-8). Let love be genuine; hate what is evil, hold fast to what is good; love one another with brotherly affection; outdo one another in showing honor. Never flag in zeal, be aglow with the Spirit, serve the Lord. Rejoice in your hope, be patient in tribulation, be constant in prayer. Contribute to the needs of the saints, practice hospitality. Bless those who persecute you; bless and do not curse them. Rejoice with those who rejoice, weep with those who weep. Live in harmony with one another; do not be haughty, but associate with the lowly; never be conceited. Repay no one evil for evil, but take thought for what is noble in the sight of all. If possible, so far as it depends upon you, live peaceably with all. Beloved, never avenge yourselves, but leave it to the wrath of God; for it is written, "Vengeance is mine, I will repay, says the Lord." No, "if your enemy is hungry, feed him or her; if they are thirsty, give them drink; for by so doing you will heap burning coals upon their heads." Do not be overcome by evil, but overcome evil with good (Rom 12:9-21).

Doubtless, any number of times all of us have heard the first passage quoted above read at weddings. One may want to rest with J. L. McKenzie's observation, "Commentators generally despair of adding any light to this luminous passage; it is that commentary on the first and greatest commandment which makes all other commentary unnecessary."[30] It is a remarkable commentary on love. The qualities of patience and kindness, of the lack of jealousy, arrogance, rudeness, irritability and resentment, look to the treatment of one's neighbor. Control over boastfulness, and insisting on one's own way, look more directly to the Christian who is reflecting on love; the same is true about rejoicing in the right and love's capability to bear,

---

[30]J. L. McKenzie, *Light on the Epistles: A Reader's Guide* (Notre Dame: Fides/Claretian, 1978) 69.

believe, hope and endure everything. "Love never ends," a phrase which is sometimes neglected in explanations of this passage, reminds us that in love itself there is nothing which makes it temporary. Our passions, weakness, and lack of virtue kill love; in itself, it is forever.

A correct understanding of Rom 12:9-21 requires the right interpretation of v 20, "No, 'if your enemy is hungry, feed him; if he is thirsty, give him drink; for by so doing you will heap burning coals on his head.'" In the next verse, the Roman Christians are given the general norm, to overcome evil with good, and that is what is described in v 20. They are to continue to do good and follow the previous instruction (v 19) to leave vengeance to the Lord. Paul's thought is not that the Christians ought to act this way so that God will take vengeance on their enemies. Such a view goes contrary to the whole idea of the pericope. It is best to follow the direction of the majority of scholars and consider the "burning coals" as the fire of remorse brought about by the consistent good deeds of the Christians.[31] The following additional points are of interest to our present study. "Let love be genuine" (v 9) is almost a heading for what follows in the rest of the chapter. Paul seems to give an explanation of what this exhortation involves. Moreover, E. Best accurately claims that vv 9-13,15-16 treat the more personal dealings of Christians with one another, and vv 14,17-21 those with non-Christians.[32] Consequently, Rom 12:9-21 is a reflection on the conduct that genuine love demands among Christians themselves and, then, with non-Christians.

Paul makes a number of other statements about love. In the next section we will examine his assertion that faith works through love (Gal 5:6). Here we note that Paul reminds Christians that they are called to freedom not as an opportunity for

---

[31]For example, see W. Barclay, *The Letter to the Romans* (The Daily Study Bible; Philadelphia, Westminister, 1957) 184; K. Barth, *The Epistle to the Romans* (New York: Oxford, 1968) 471-5; C. K. Barrett, *The Epistle to the Romans* (HNTC; New York: Harper & Row, 1957) 242-3; E. Best, *The Letter of Paul to the Romans* (The Cambridge Bible Commentary; Cambridge: University, 1967) 146; J. Huby & S. Lyonnet, *Saint Paul: Epître aux Romains* (VSX; Paris: Beauchesne, 1957) 428-30; M. J. Lagrange, *Saint Paul: Epître aux Romains* (EBib; Paris: J. Gabalda, 1916) 308-9.

[32]E. Best, *Romans*, 143-4.

the flesh, but through love to be servants of one another (Gal 5:13). Christian freedom is intended for loving service.

Knowledge puffs up, but love builds up (1 Cor 8:1).[33] For example, a Christian is not walking in love if his brother or sister is injured by what is eaten (Rom 14:15). Moreover, Christians can always increase their love. Thus, Paul prays that the Lord may make the Thessalonians increase and abound in love for one another and for everyone, as Paul, Silas and Timothy do for them (1 Thess 3:12;4:9-10). Again, Paul offers a similar prayer for the Philippians; this time he asks that the increase of their love may abound with knowledge and all discernment that they may approve what is excellent and likewise be pure and blameless on the day of the Lord, filled with the fruits of righteousness (Phil 1:9-11).[34]

Paul speaks often of his own love and that of his communities. He tells the Corinthians that his love is with all of them in Christ Jesus (1 Cor 16:24). When he explains to them why he does not accept their financial support, he concludes with the words, "And why? Because I do not love you? God knows I do!" (2 Cor 11:11; cf. 6:6). Concerned about his third visit to Corinth, Paul asks, "If I love you the more, am I to be loved the less?" (2 Cor 12:15). Paul justifies his feelings for the Philippians because he holds them in his heart and God knows how he yearns for all of them with the affection of Christ Jesus (Phil 1:7-8). Later he writes that even if he is to be poured out as a libation for their faith, he is glad and rejoices, and they ought to do the same with him (Phil 2:17-18). The Philippians are Paul's brothers and sisters whom he loves and longs for, his joy and crown. He did not seek their gift of financial support, but its fruit which increases to their credit (Phil 4:1,17).

---

[33]Romano Penna ("'La carità edifica', aspetti ecclesiologici dell'agape in San Paolo," *Lateranum* 51 [1985] 18) points out that Paul's exhortations to love are regularly generic. Only twice, is Paul specific: the passages about the weak (1 Cor 8; Rom 14:1-15:13) and those on ministries (cf. 1 Cor 12-14; Rom 12:3-10; Eph 4:11-16).

[34]George T. Montague (*Growth in Christ: A Study in Paul's Theology of Progress* [Fribourg: St. Paul's, 1961] 3-20,63-9,112-35,165-258) sees a theology of progress in the following passages relevant to our study: 1 Thess 3:10-13;5:23f; 1 Cor 3:1-3;13:10-12;14:20; 2 Cor 3:9; Rom 15:5f,13; Phil 1:9-11;3:10-16.

Although Paul could command Philemon, for love's sake he prefers to appeal to him on Onesimus' behalf. Onesimus is Paul's beloved brother and in sending him back he is sending his very heart. Paul himself will make good anything Onesimus might owe Philemon (Phlm 8-10,12,16-19).

Love also characterizes the Pauline communities. Paul and his companions thankfully remember before God the labor of the Thessalonians' love (1 Thess 1:3). In his encouragement to the Corinthians to participate in the collection, Paul argues that since they excel in everything, including their love for Timothy and himself, they should also excel in this gracious work, the collection, which will be a proof of their love (2 Cor 8:7-18,24). Earlier, Paul begged the Corinthians to re-affirm their love for the man who had been excommunicated from the community lest he be overwhelmed by excessive sorrow (2 Cor 2:7-8). Those who preach Christ from good will while Paul is in prison, do it out of love (Phil 1:16). The Philippians' financial support of Paul demonstrates their concern for him.[35] Their repeated help in Thessalonica was an example of this. Epaphroditus, and the gifts he brought, were a fragrant offering, a sacrifice acceptable and pleasing to God (Phil 4:10,14-18; cf. 2:25-30). On the other hand, Paul has no one like Timothy who is genuinely anxious for the Philippians' welfare (Phil 2:20). Finally, Paul thanks God for Philemon's love from which Paul derives much joy and comfort because through it the hearts of the saints have been refreshed. Now Philemon should receive Onesimus back as a beloved brother, as Paul himself; in fact, Paul is confident that Philemon will do even more than he is asked (Phlm 4-7,16-17,21).

For Paul, love is the criterion for determining what a Christian should do in a given situation. We owe love to everyone else, and its ultimate result will be good. The qualities of Christian love govern our relationship to other Christians, non-Christians and ourselves. Love endures forever, and Chris-

---

[35]J. Paul Sampley (*Pauline Partnership in Christ: Christian Community and Commitment* [Philadelphia: Fortress, 1980] 51-115) contends that, with the Philippians alone of all his churches, Paul entered into a partnership (*societas*) so fully that he accepted their financial support for his preaching as their representative.

tian freedom is an opportunity to serve one another in love. Love builds up and can always be increased, and is found in the lives of Paul and his communities.[36]

Faith

In general, Christians are agreed that for Paul salvation is only obtained through faith, which itself is a gift of God. There is no given human action we can perform on our own that will bring salvation. Certainly, this is Roman Catholic teaching. Unfortunately, this very description of Pauline faith has led to a tendency to isolate it from Christian living. Yet for Paul, "faith," of which "obedience" can be a synonym, most correctly means the responsive trust of the whole human person in Christ and the Father. This probably also explains why Paul does not often speak of our love of God because such love is included in faith itself.

Faith should not be isolated from Christian living or morality. For whatever does not proceed from faith is sin, and so we should act out of faith (Rom 14:23; Phil 1:27).[37] A number of times Paul has connected faith with love. The clearest statement of this is found in Galatians, "For in Christ Jesus neither circumcision nor uncircumcision is of any avail, but faith working through love" (Gal 5:6). Faith is listed beside love (and hope) in 1 Thess 1:3;3:6; 1 Cor 13:13; Phlm 5. All of these latter citations suggest a relationship between faith and Christian moral living. The first citation speaks of the "work of faith"; the second occurs in a section which speaks of spiritual gifts which are for the common good (1 Cor 12:7; cf Gal 5:22-23; 2 Cor 8:7), and lastly, Paul writes of Philemon's love and faith which "you have toward the Lord Jesus and all the saints." Philemon's faith bears on his actions toward his fellow

---

[36]For further reading on "love" in Paul, see P. Perkins, *Love Commands in the New Testament* (New York: Paulist, 1982) 66-96. Confer also T. J. Deidun, *New Covenant Morality in Paul* (AB 89; Rome: Biblical Institute, 1981) 100-85,218-26,249-50.

[37]J-N. Aletti, "L'ethicisation de l'Esprit Saint," 123-42.

Christians. A Pauline connection between faith and moral living, especially love, is confirmed by 1 Cor 16:13-14: "Be watchful, stand firm in your faith, be courageous, be strong. Let all that you do be done in love."

Paul describes the present life of the Corinthians and himself with the words, "for we walk by faith, not by sight" (2 Cor 5:7). Of himself, Paul says, ". . .and the life I now live in the flesh I live by faith in the Son of God" (Gal 2:20; cf. 3:11; Rom 1:17). Again, this is true of the Corinthians because Paul responds to one of their charges, "Not that we lord it over your faith; we work with you for your joy, for you stand firm in your faith" (2 Cor 1:24). "To stand firm in one's faith" seems to be a summary of Christian existence.

From what has been said thus far, an insight can be gained into the meaning of Rom 12:3:

> For by the grace given to me I bid everyone among you not to think of himself or herself more highly than he or she ought to think, but to think with sober judgment, each according to the measure of faith which God has assigned.

The passage goes on to speak of the different gifts in the body. Consequently, God has given faith to all Christians, but in different measures; one's gift and task are related to his or her measure of faith.

Faith leads to speaking the gospel message (2 Cor 4:13-15) which surely is a good deed. Consequently, God's gift of faith should not be isolated from Paul's morality. In fact, all good actions ought to flow from it. Faith works through love and is associated with it. Christians live by faith and stand firm in it. One's faith bears on one's spiritual gifts.

Hope

As already noted, hope is connected by Paul with love and faith. Love hopes all things (1 Cor 13:7). How Paul joins faith and hope is best seen in Rom 5:1-5 (cf. Gal 5:5) where faith leads to justification, peace, access to grace and hope of sharing

God's glory. Christians can boast of their suffering, which produces endurance, then character, and then hope. Consequently, faith ultimately brings hope. Rom 8:18-25 also speak of this hope in the midst of suffering. The hope is in the resurrection and in being sons and daughters of God. Since one does not hope in that which is seen, Christians wait in patience. About the resurrection, Paul says, "If for this life only we have hoped in Christ, we are most to be pitied"(1 Cor 15:19).

The OT writings mentioned in Rom 15:4 are instructional, so that by patience and encouragement we would have hope. Of course, God is the source of hope (2 Cor 1:10), and Paul prays that the God of hope might fill the Roman Christians with all joy and peace in believing so that by the power of the Holy Spirit they may abound in hope (Rom 15:12-13). They are to rejoice in hope (Rom 12:12). Christian hope makes us bold not to veil what God has done in the new dispensation (2 Cor 3:12), and in this spirit, Paul hopes that the Corinthians' faith increases and that his missionary field among them be enlarged so that he and his companions might preach in lands further on (2 Cor 10:15-16). Hope in the resurrection should keep Christians from grieving as do others who have no such hope (1 Thess 4:13).

Hope touches other aspects of Christian living. Paul thanks God for the Thessalonians' hope (1 Thess 1:3). He calls them his hope, joy, and crown of boasting at the coming of the Lord, seemingly because of his satisfaction at their response to his preaching (1 Thess 2:19). They are to put on the helmet of the hope of salvation since they are of the day, and are sons and daughters of the light (1 Thess 5:8). Paul's hope in the Corinthians is firm, for as they share in his suffering, so they will share in his comfort. He also hopes that they will fully understand his letters, and relates this understanding, too, to the day of the Lord (2 Cor 1:7,13-14).

Paul, in prison, hopes that he will not at all be ashamed, but that with full courage now as always Christ will be honored in his body (Phil 1:20). He hopes in the Lord to send Timothy soon to the Philippians (Phil 2:19,23), and he even speaks of Christian hope as regards his forthcoming visits to his communities (1 Cor 16:7; Rom 15:24; Phlm 22).

Christians hope in God and in Christ, in the resurrection, in being sons and daughters of God; one does not hope in what one sees, nor with it need one grieve. Hope characterizes the whole of Christian life; it touches on the scriptures, on imprisonment, on the struggle with evil, and on personal interactions. Hope flows from faith and is an expression of love. Through hope Christians rejoice in hard times and develop patience, endurance and character. Hope should be firm and lead to bold proclamation.

Peace, Joy and Comfort

Unity with Christ has already been seen to be a source of Christian morality. To be associated with that unity is peace, for "peace" can be the equivalent of reconciliation (e.g. Rom 5:1). In fact, peace characterizes Christian living. God calls us to peace (1 Cor 7:15). To set one's mind on the Spirit is life and peace (Rom 8:6; Gal 5:22), and the Kingdom of God is not food and drink, but righteousness, peace and joy in the Spirit (Rom 14:17). Paul wishes peace on the Christians who live by the rule of the new creation (Gal 6:16). Christians are to live at peace and in harmony with one another (1 Thess 5:13; 2 Cor 13:11; Rom 12:16,18), so they may with one voice glorify the God and Father of our Lord Jesus Christ (Rom 15:5-6). They are to pursue what makes for peace and for mutual upbuilding (Rom 14:19).

Sometimes peace is associated with joy (Rom 14:17;15:13; Gal 5:22). Christians are to rejoice always (1 Thess 5:16; cf. 2 Cor 6:10; Phil 3:1;4:4). Despite persecution, the Thessalonians receive the word with the joy of the Spirit (1 Thess 1:6). Christians rejoice in hope (Rom 12:12). Their love does not rejoice at wrong, but in the right (1 Cor 13:6). If one member of the body is honored, all rejoice together (1 Cor 12:26). In this same spirit, the Roman Christians are instructed to rejoice with those who rejoice and to weep with those who weep (Rom 12:15).

Christians experience joy in one another. Paul has joy because of the Thessalonians (1 Thess 3:9), the Corinthians (2

Cor 2:2-2;7:4), the Romans (16:19), and the Philippians (e.g. 4:1). Paul rejoices at the coming of Stephanas, Fortunatus and Achaicus, because they have made up for the Corinthians' absence (1 Cor 16:17). The "Letter of Tears" occasions both grief and joy for Paul, and for the Corinthians (2 Cor 2:1-4; 7:5-16). He wrote because he did not want to suffer pain from those who should make him rejoice, and because he is convinced that his joy is the joy of them all. Paul does not rejoice because his letter grieved them, but because they grieved unto repenting. He likewise rejoices at Titus' joy in finding everything among the Corinthians to be just as Paul had told him. Paul rejoices because he has perfect confidence in the Corinthians. Finally, Paul asks the Romans to pray that the collection might be accepted by the saints in Jerusalem, so that he might come to them with joy and be refreshed in their company (Rom 15:31-32).

It is common knowledge that "rejoicing" is a significant theme in Paul's Letter to the Philippians. Although he is in prison, Paul rejoices that Christ is proclaimed (1:18-19). The Philippians should complete Paul's joy by being of the same mind (2:2). Even if he is poured out as a libation upon the sacrificial offering of the Philippians' faith, Paul is glad and rejoices with them all; they should be glad and rejoice with him (2:17-18). The Philippians are Paul's joy and crown (4:1), and their revived concern for him causes him to rejoice greatly in the Lord (4:10). Finally, Paul derives much joy and comfort from Philemon's love because through it the saints have been refreshed (Phlm 7).

The grace of God in the churches of Macedonia results in their abundant joy, overflowing in liberality for the collection, despite their affliction and poverty (2 Cor 8:1-5). Paul contends that he does not lord it over the Corinthians' faith, but works with them for their joy, for they stand firm in faith (2 Cor 1:24). He is all the more eager to send Epaphroditus back to the Philippians, that they may rejoice at seeing him again, since he was sick. Paul instructs the Philippians to receive him with all joy, and to honor such men, for he risked his life for the work of Christ and the Philippians' service of Paul.

"Comfort" relates to peace and joy. Paul is comforted by

Timothy's news of the Thessalonians' faith (1 Thess 3:7), and directs them to comfort one another with their belief in a resurrection (1 Thess 4:18). The theme of comfort is stronger in 2 Corinthians. Paul tells the Corinthians to forgive and comfort the man whom they had excommunicated (2:7). Whether this man was the cause or not, Paul had been involved in a very unpleasant disagreement with the Corinthians which, immediately prior to this letter, reached a happy solution. So Paul ten times writes of comfort in the midst of affliction and sufferings (1:3-7). Titus' coming to Macedonia, and the comfort he derived from his visit to the Corinthians, were also a comfort to Paul, whose letter to them led to repentance. Their evident zeal brings Paul comfort (7:4-16).

Holiness

Surely, "being made holy" (e.g. 1 Cor 1:2;6:11), "holiness" (1 Cor 1:30), and being a "saint" (e.g. Rom 1:7;8:27;12:13;15:25-26,31) are ways of speaking of Pauline salvation. But "holiness" also looks to Christian living and moral activity (2 Cor 7:1; Phil 4:8; cf. 1:17). Paul ministers in holiness (2 Cor 6:6) and wishes that the Lord make the Thessalonians abound in love for one another, and everyone, so that their hearts are established as unblamable in holiness before our God and Father, at the coming of our Lord Jesus with all his saints (1 Thess 3:11-13). The Corinthians' grief over the misunderstanding between Paul and themselves led to the right attitudes, and they have shown themselves to be holy and blameless in the matter (2 Cor 7:11). Paul has betrothed them as a pure bride to her one husband, Christ (2 Cor 11:2-3).

Paul's contention, "And the unmarried woman or girl is anxious about the affairs of the Lord, how to be holy in body and spirit," sees holiness as a reference to all of Christian living (1 Cor 7:34). Even though the exhortation in 2 Cor 7:1, "Since we have these promises, beloved, let us cleanse ourselves from every defilement of body and spirit, and make holiness perfect in the fear of God," may be an insertion, it does not contradict Paul's notion of holiness. Paul writes to the Romans that they are freed from sin and should now yield their members to righteousness, for holiness. They have become slaves of God; the return they get is sanctification and its end, eternal life (Rom 6:19,22). The general charge to the Romans is "to present your bodies as a living sacrifice, holy and acceptable to God, which is your spiritual worship. . . . " (Rom 12:1).[38]

Holiness, for Paul, can bear on one's attitude toward sexuality. True, 1 Thess 4:1-8 cannot be understood without reference to the general statement on holiness in 3:13-4:1, but 4:2-8 reviews Paul's precepts for the Thessalonian men. They are to strive for holiness (vv 3-4,7) by abstaining from unchastity, taking a wife in holiness and honor, and not wronging their brother in this matter.

Service and Ministry

Service and ministry are part of Christian living. Paul expresses these ideas in a number of ways, and probably only "slavery" needs to be singled out as having a more specific meaning. Generally speaking, there is a variety of service but the same Lord (1 Cor 12:5), and as Paul bluntly observes, service is to be used for serving (Rom 12:7). Both the whole of the old covenant and of the new can be referred to as "ministry" or "service," although most modern translations of 2 Cor 3:6-11 obscure this fact.

"Slavery" probably looks to a more intense expression of service. A slave's dedication to the master has to be total. This is why Paul says that if he sought to please human beings he

[38]As regards Rom 12:1, Raymond Corriveau (*The Liturgy of Life: A Study of the Ethical Thought of St. Paul in His Letters to the Early Christian Communities,* Montréal: Les Editions Bellarmin, 1970, 19-185) makes interesting reading. Corriveau treats 1 Thess 1:9; 1 Cor 3:16f;5:6-8;6:19f; 2 Cor 2:14f;6:16-7:1;9:12; Rom 1:9;12:1;15:16 and Phil 2:17;4:18b as major texts in Paul's epistles which represent the daily life of the Christian as a worship of God. Likewise, Michael Newton (*The Concept of Purity at Qumran and in the Letters of Paul* [Cambridge: University, 1985] 1-9,52-116) relates purity and the cult in the letters of Paul to the Christian community as the Temple (1 Cor 3:16f;6:19; 2 Cor 6:16-7:1), to Paul as priest to the community, to the believer as both sacrificial offering and priest and to membership and the continuing life of the Church.

would not be a slave of Christ (Gal 1:10; cf. 1 Thess 2:4) and that one is either a slave of sin or a slave of faith (Rom 6:16; cf. 16:18; 1 Thess 1:9). We are no longer slaves to fear, corruption and false gods; we have received the spirit of children of God, and are known by him (Rom 8:15,21; Gal 4:8-9,24-25;5:1). We are no longer enslaved to sin, but to righteousness (Rom 6:6,17,20;14:17-18), and we should be aglow with the Spirit and serve the Lord (Rom 12:11; cf. 7:6). Through love, we should be slaves of one another (Gal 5:13). Moreover, physical slavery is not that significant, since in Christ the slave becomes free, and the free man or woman becomes Christ's slave (1 Cor 7:21-23; cf. 1 Cor 12:13; Gal 3:27-28; Phlm 16). Paul copies the tradition that Jesus takes on the form of a slave (Phil 2:7), and describes himself and Timothy as slaves of Christ Jesus (Phil 1:1;2:22; 2 Cor 4:5; Gal 1:10).

Ministry and service can be spoken of in other ways. Christ can be called a minister (Rom 15:8; cf. Gal 2:17), and the notion of ministry is predicated of a number of people. God makes Timothy and Paul competent to be ministers (2 Cor 3:6;4:1;11:23), and Paul designates Apollos and himself as ministers (1 Cor 3:5). Stephanas and his household have devoted themselves to the service of the saints (1 Cor 16:15). The address of the Letter to the Philippians speaks of "bishops" and deacons, or ministers (1:1), and Phoebe is a deaconess (Rom 16:1). Finally, even governing authorities are, in a sense, ministers of God (Rom 13:4).

Some additional comments from Paul assist us in understanding how we ought to perceive ministry. Because of it, Paul does not lose heart but openly states the truth, and thus recommends himself to everyone's conscience (2 Cor 4:1-2). Paul puts no obstacle in anyone's way, so that no fault may be found with his ministry (2 Cor 6:3); this is the reason why he does not take any money for his ministry to the Corinthians (1 Cor 9:12; cf. 9:3-18). He becomes everything to everyone, that he might save some, and he does it for the gospel, to share in its blessing (1 Cor 9:19-23; cf. 10:33). A minister must be faithful, and leave the judgment of his or her performance to God. Ministers should not be puffed up, and ought to be willing to become fools for Christ's sake (1 Cor 4:1-13). Elsewhere, this latter becomes identified with dying and rising with Christ (cf. 2 Cor 4:7-16;6:3-10). Finally, ministry as a concept can apparently embrace whatever one does for the gospel. Paul calls his service of the Corinthian church (2 Cor 11:8; cf. 3:3), reconciliation (2 Cor 5:18) and the collection (2 Cor 8:4,19-20;9:1,12-13; Rom 15:25,31) all "ministry."

Work and Labor

"Work" or "labor" are other ways of speaking of Christian living (1 Cor 15:58; Phil 2:12-13). Of course, "work" and "labor" can refer to evil deeds, as well as to good ones.[39] There seems to be no need to refer to the Greek words used, but I will use "work" or "labor" in this presentation. Paul's reader is not surprised to learn that there are varieties of works, but that the same God works them all in everyone (1 Cor 12:6; cf. 2 Cor 5:5;9:8). Paul and Apollos are God's fellow workers in Corinth (1 Cor 3:9), and Timothy and Paul are doing the work of the Lord (1 Cor 16:10). Paul does not boast, except in what Christ has worked through him to win obedience from the Gentiles, by word and labor (Rom 15:18). Christian faith works through love (Gal 5:6), and love does not work evil against one's neighbor (Rom 13:10). While we have the opportunity, we are to work the good for everyone, especially for those of the household of faith (Gal 6:10).

Paul writes of his own works or labors (2 Cor 6:5;10:11). He recalls for the Thessalonians his labor and toil, and how he worked among them day and night, so as to burden none of them (1 Thess 2:9; cf. 1 Cor 4:12;9:6-18). He works the signs of a true apostle for the Corinthians (2 Cor 12:12; cf. Rom 15:18-19); in fact, they are his workmanship in the Lord (1 Cor 9:1). Paul feels that in reality he works *with* the Corinthians (2 Cor 1:24). Life in the flesh means fruitful labor for him among the Philippians (1:22). He writes to the Romans in a bold fashion because of the grace given him by God to be a worker of

---

[39]For examples of references to evil deeds, see 1 Cor 5:2f; 2 Cor 11:13,15; Gal 5:19; Phil 3:2; Rom 2:9;7:5-20;13:12.

Christ Jesus for the Gentiles, in the priestly labor of the gospel of God (Rom 15:16). Paul can contend that, through the grace of God, he has worked harder than any of the other apostles (1 Cor 15:10), and that he has performed far greater labors than the false apostles in Corinth (2 Cor 11:23; cf vv 21-29). He is willing to give his life in priestly labors for the Philippians' faith (Phil 2:17). Yet, he still fears that he may have labored in vain among some of his communities (1 Thess 3:5; Gal 4:11; cf. Phil 2:16).

Paul speaks of his fellow workers.[40] Mary, Tryphaena and Tryphosa are called workers (Rom 16:6,12). Epaphroditus labors on behalf of Paul's needs, and nearly dies for the work of Christ (Phil 2:25,30). Later, in the same letter, Paul asks his "true yokefellow" to help Euodia and Syntyche, for they have labored side by side with Paul in the gospel together with Clement and the other workers associated with him, whose names are in the book of life (Phil 4:2f). Philemon is Paul's beloved fellow worker, and Archippus his fellow soldier (Phlm 1b-2). All such laborers deserve recognition.

Paul thanks God for the Thessalonians' work of faith and labor of love (1 Thess 1:3). Each of the Galatians is instructed to test his or her own work (Gal 6:4). "Labor" and "work" are also used by Paul of one good Christian action which leads to another. Godly grief works repentance for the Corinthians (2 Cor 7:10-11); the collection, thanksgiving to God (2 Cor 9:11-12). Suffering works endurance (Rom 5:3; cf. 2 Cor 1:6;4:17), whereas Philemon's faith works knowledge of good (Phlm 6). Finally, physical labor becomes Christians, for Paul exhorts the Thessalonians, "to aspire to live quietly, to mind your own affairs, to work with your hands, as we charged you; so that you may command the respect of outsiders, and be dependent on nobody" (1 Thess 4:11-12). Ultimately, there will be glory, honor and peace for everyone whose works are good (Rom 2:10), and we will all be judged by our works (1 Cor 3:13-15;15:58; cf. Rom 2:6-7).

---

[40]2 Cor 6:1;8:23; Phil 2:25;4:3; Phlm 1,24; Rom 16:3,9,21.

Preaching the Gospel, Proclamation and Teaching

Perhaps this section is best begun by referring to Rom 10:14f, which state in a common-sense manner the Christian need and significance of proclamation:

> But how are human beings to call upon him in whom they have not believed? And how are they to believe in him of whom they have never heard? And how are they to hear without a preacher? And how can they preach unless they are sent? As it is written, "How beautiful are the feet of those who preach good news!"

The marvel is that the former persecutor Paul was commissioned by God to preach the gospel (1 Thess 2:4; Gal 1:15f,23; Rom 1:1). Although in the context he is obviously trying to correct misunderstanding about baptism, yet Paul can write, "For Christ did not send me to baptize but to preach the gospel...." (1 Cor 1:17). He feels obligated to preach to the Gentiles and barbarians and is eager to do so (Rom 1:14-16). Preaching the gospel does not lead Paul to boast, rather it is a necessity and his reward is to do so free of charge (1 Cor 9:16-18; cf. 1 Thess 2:9; 2 Cor 11:7), even though he could enjoy the benefits of the Lord's command that those who proclaim the gospel should thereby get their living (1 Cor 9:14). Paul preaches the true gospel (1 Thess 2:4-7; 2 Cor 11:4; Gal 1:6-12;2:5); later in life, he confirms this gospel to the Gentiles with those in Jerusalem, lest somehow he should be or had run in vain (Gal 2:2). Nonetheless, his gospel was not from any human being (Gal 1:6-12).

The gospel that Paul preaches to the Thessalonians is not only in words, but also in power and in the Holy Spirit and with full conviction (1 Thess 1:5; Rom 15:15-21). In the midst of opposition, Paul and his companions not only share the gospel, but themselves (1 Thess 2:2,8). However, not all was glorious. Paul originally spoke to the Galatians because he was suffering from a bodily ailment (Gal 4:13), and his preaching of the gospel among the Corinthians was not with eloquent wisdom, lest the cross of Christ be emptied of its power (1 Cor

1:16; cf. 2:1-5; 2 Cor 10:10f;11:6). Finally, Paul's tremendous preaching activity is in part explained by the fact that he does not want to build on another's foundation (Rom 15:17-21; 2 Cor 10:15f).

Others, besides Paul, preach the gospel. From the beginning, the Philippians share in Paul's proclamation of the gospel and in its defense and confirmation (Phil 1:5-7;4:15-20), and Timothy is Paul's fellow worker for the gospel (1 Thess 3:2; Phil 2:22).

Proclamation (*kerygma*) is frequently the equivalent of preaching the gospel (cf. 1 Cor 1:21;2:4;15:11,14; Rom 16:25) and, not surprisingly, is found in the same context (1 Thess 2:9; Gal 2:2; Phil 1:15). Paul asks the Corinthians, in response to their inquiry, if Christ is proclaimed as raised from the dead, how can some of them say that there is no resurrection of the dead (1 Cor 15:12). Paul and his companions proclaim the word of faith (1 Cor 10:8; cf. vv 14f) and Christ crucified, a stumbling block to Jews and folly to the Gentiles (1 Cor 1:23; cf. Gal 5:11). They proclaim the Son of God, Jesus Christ, who was not Yes and No, but always Yes because all the promises of God find their Yes in him (2 Cor 1:19f). They do not preach themselves, but Jesus Christ as Lord, with themselves as the Corinthians' servant for Jesus' sake (2 Cor 4:5). Of himself, Paul humbly says that he pommels his body and subdues it, lest after proclaiming to others he himself be disqualified (1 Cor 9:27).

Even the ordinary word, "to speak" can mean the Christian activity of proclaiming the gospel.[41] Paul believes and so he speaks to the Corinthians that grace might extend to more and more people and increase thanksgiving to God (2 Cor 4:13-15). Often enough, "to speak" is used in the same context as preaching the gospel (1 Thess 2:2,4; Phil 1:14; Rom 15:8), but this is far from always the case. The word of the Lord and the faith among the Thessalonians is so well known that Paul does not have to speak to them about these (1 Thess 1:8). The

---

[41]This also appears to be somewhat true of "I say" (*legō*), e.g., 1 Cor 12:3;15:51; Rom 15:8.

Thessalonians have opponents just as Paul has Jewish opponents who prevent him from speaking to the Gentiles that they may be saved (1 Thess 2:16).

Among the mature at Corinth, Paul speaks the hidden wisdom of God, which is not of this world (1 Cor 2:6f). He speaks in words not taught by human wisdom but by the Spirit (1 Cor 2:13). In the past Paul could not speak to them as spiritual persons because they were of the flesh and babes in Christ. Their present strife and jealousy indicates that they are still of the flesh (1 Cor 3:1-4). The conduct of Paul and his companions toward the Corinthians is exemplary. They are not peddlers of God's word, but men of sincerity, commissioned by God, who speak in Christ (2 Cor 2:17; cf. 7:14). They speak everything for the building up of their beloved Corinthians (2 Cor 12:19).

Two passages demonstrate that "to speak," in the above sense, can also be used of the Christians in general. "No one speaking by the Spirit of God ever says 'Jesus be cursed' and no one can say 'Jesus is Lord' except by the Holy Spirit (1 Cor 12:3). Unfortunately, the second example likewise reveals the social limitations of the times. In liturgical assemblies, designed to nourish the faith, women are not to speak (1 Cor 14:34f).

Teaching is a gift in the body of Christ and is listed third, after apostleship and prophecy, as a function of certain members of the community (Rom 12:7; cf. 1 Cor 12:28f). Of course, nature itself (1 Cor 11:14), and whatever is written in the OT can teach Christians (Rom 15:4). But as a function of an individual Christian, teaching like the other gifts is to be used to build up one's fellow members (1 Cor 14:26; v 6). Paul himself teaches (1 Cor 4:17; cf. 14:19). More practically and with application to all Christians, the one who is taught the word should share all good things with the teacher (Gal 6:6).

Prophecy and Speaking in Tongues

Most reasonably, Paul's notion of prophecy flows out of that of the Old Testament (1 Thess 2:15; Rom 1:2-4;3:21f;11:2-4;16:26). Christian prophecy is a gift of the Spirit (1 Cor 12:10;

Rom 12:6) and a function of the body, second only to apostleship (1 Cor 12:28f). This gift is given in proportion to one's
faith (Rom 12:6) and is to be subordinated to love (1 Cor
13:2). In fact, prophecy is imperfect and passes away (1 Cor
13:8f). Nonetheless, prophesying is not to be despised (1 Thess
5:20).

Paul has an insightful commentary on prophecy and speaking in tongues in 1 Cor 14:1-40. Prophecy, which depends on
revelations, can be superior to speaking in tongues because it
speaks to human beings for their upbuilding, encouragement
and consolation. It involves the minds of others and builds up
the Church. Likewise, it can reveal the secrets of one's heart,
and thus, everyone can learn. The Corinthians ought to desire
earnestly to prophesy (cf. 1 Cor 11:4f), but those who think
they are prophets should acknowledge that what Paul writes is
a command of God. Consequently, everything should be done
in order, for God is not a God of confusion but of peace.

Good order is also a criterion for whether one should speak
in tongues or not. Like prophecy, speaking in tongues is a gift
of the Spirit (1 Cor 12:10,28,30) which is subordinate to love
(1 Cor 13:1). After all, tongues will cease (1 Cor 13:8). Actually,
Paul wants everyone to speak in tongues, and he himself does
so more than any of the Corinthians. So, speaking in tongues
is not to be forbidden. Yet, this gift presents certain problems.
Whoever speaks in tongues relates mysteries in the Spirit and
edifies himself or herself, but what is said is not intelligible.
Others are not instructed. Most reasonably, the one who
speaks in tongues should pray for the power of interpretation,
itself a gift of the Spirit (1 Cor 12:10,30). Two or, at most,
three should speak in tongues. If there is no interpreter, there
should be silence, for the principle of building up the community likewise governs this gift.

Humility, Meekness, Fear and Trembling

Paul calls Christians to be humble and meek and to work
out their salvation in fear and trembling. Previously, it was
noted that Paul in Phil 2:1-5 encourages harmony in the

community by exhorting the Philippians to think the same thing in the Lord. In Phil 2:6-11, Christ Jesus becomes an example of humility for Christians. Although in the form of God, he was not selfish but emptied himself, took on the form of a servant and humbled himself even to the extent of death on the cross.

The essence of humility is to realize who God is and who we are, as Paul does when he confesses that he and his companions hold the treasure of the gospel in earthen vessels to show that the transcendent power belongs to God and not to them (2 Cor 4:7). Paul humbles himself to exalt the Corinthians because he preaches God's gospel to them without cost (2 Cor 11:7). He says about his own ability to deal with want and abundance that he knows how to be humble and how to abound (Phil 4:12). Yet God can humble one, and that is exactly what Paul fears may be the result of his third visit to the Corinthians (2 Cor 12:21).

Paul's general principle for Christians is that they should live in harmony with one another and not be haughty, but associate with the humble and never be conceited (Rom 12:16). For if anyone thinks that he or she is something, when they are nothing, they deceive themselves (Gal 6:3). Paul bids the Romans not to think of themselves more highly than is appropriate; each should think with sober judgment, according to the measure of faith that God has assigned him or her (Rom 12:3). They should not be proud because God has grafted them onto the olive tree, while the natural branches were cut away; rather they should stand in reverential fear. It is a mystery: a hardening has come upon part of Israel, until the full number of the Gentiles come in, and so all Israel will be saved. However, if God did not spare the natural branches, neither will he spare the Christians, if they are not receptive of his kindness (Rom 11:17-27). A consolation is that God comforts the humble (2 Cor 7:6).

According to Paul, the Corinthians were particularly puffed up or arrogant. While in their midst he experienced weakness, fear and much trembling, and was humble (1 Cor 2:3; 2 Cor 7:5;10:1,10). But the Corinthians are puffed up. They should learn from the example of Apollos and Paul not to go beyond what is written, that none of them may be puffed up in favor of one against another. Paul's visit will discover not the talk of those who are puffed up but their power (1 Cor 4:6,18f; cf. 2 Cor 10:5). What do they wish? Is he to come to them with a rod, or with love in a spirit of meekness (1 Cor 4:21)? Since "spirit of meekness" ends that chapter and section, it is clear that such is the way Paul chooses to come. Again, the Corinthians are puffed up about their tolerance for the man who is living with his father's wife. They ought to be mourning (1 Cor 5:2). Their knowledge about their freedom to eat meat offered to idols has puffed them up, too. So, Paul proclaims that love builds up and is not boastful, puffed up or rude (1 Cor 13:4f). Even at the end of 2 Cor (12: 20f), Paul is fearful about his third visit and the possibility that he may still find the Corinthians to be puffed up and unrepentant.

However, Paul does not find arrogance and selfishness only among the Corinthians. To the Philippians he writes that he has no one like Timothy, for the others look after their own interests, not those of Jesus Christ (cf. Phil 2:19-21).

Meekness and gentleness are qualities that Christ shares with the Christians (2 Cor 10:1). Meekness is a fruit of the Spirit (Gal 5:23). If anyone is overtaken in any trespass, the Galatians who are spiritual should restore him or her in a spirit of meekness and look to themselves, lest they should be tempted (Gal 6:1; cf. 1 Cor 4:21). The Philippians are to let their gentleness be known to everyone (Phil 4:5).

Perhaps, "fear" (*phobos*), would be better translated as "reverential fear" or "awe." After all, the Roman Christians are told that they did not receive the spirit of slavery to fall back into fear, but the Spirit of being sons and daughters, by which they cry, "Abba! Father!" (Romans 8:15). Most properly, reverential fear is due to God; hence, those who are under the power of sin have no fear of God in their eyes (Rom 3:8). On the contrary, confident in the resurrection and aware of the coming judgment, Paul knows the fear of God and so persuades individuals (2 Cor 5:11). Although a possible insertion, 2 Cor 7:1 summarizes how the Corinthians should live as Christians. "Since we have these promises, beloved, let us cleanse ourselves from every defilement of body and spirit, and make holiness perfect in the fear of God." Elsewhere, Paul instructs the Philipppians to work out their salvation with fear and trembling (Phil 2:12). He is impressed how the godly grief of the Corinthians over their mutual misunderstanding led to a reverential fear, and thus with fear and trembling they received Titus (2 Cor 7:11,15).

Patience and Endurance

Of course, God is the one who is truly patient (Rom 2:4;9:22). He will give eternal life to those who by patience in well-doing seek for glory, honor and immortality (Rom 2:7). Patience is a fruit of the Spirit (Gal 5:22) and characterizes Christian love (1 Cor 13:4). God is faithful, he will not let the Christians be tempted beyond their strength but will also provide a way of escape so that they can endure it (1 Cor 10:13). Endurance produces character (Rom 5:4). By endurance and the encouragement of scriptures (OT; the NT was just being written) Christians can have hope (Rom 15:4). Moreover, since they hope for what they do not see, they wait for it with patience (Rom 8:25).

Paul and his companions in every way recommend themselves as servants of God through great endurance and patience (2 Cor 6:4,6), and with all patience, Paul performed the signs of an apostle among the Corinthians (2 Cor 12:12). He remembers in his thanksgiving the patience of the Thessalonians' hope in our Lord Jesus Christ (1 Thess 1:3). Later, in the letter, he encourages them to be patient with everyone in the community (5:14). Paul, in another thanksgiving, assures the Corinthians that, if he and Timothy are comforted, it is for the Corinthians' comfort, which they experience when they endure the same sufferings (2 Cor 1:6).

Boasting in the Lord

Whoever boasts should boast in the Lord (1 Cor 1:31; 2 Cor 10:17), for God achieves everything. Consequently, Christians boast in God through the Lord Jesus, through whom they have received reconciliation (Rom 5:11). Certain boasting is out of place. When Paul is establishing that everyone is a sinner and needs redemption, he observes that the Jews boast in the law but do not keep it (Rom 2:17,23). Also, the Corinthians are wrong to boast about the destructive incest in their midst (1 Cor 5:6); the false apostles in Corinth want to boast that they are like Paul (2 Cor 11:12-15), and opponents want to boast in the Galatians' flesh and not be persecuted for the cross of Christ (Gal 6:12f). But God has chosen what is lowly and despised to bring to nothing things that are, so that no human being might boast in his presence (1 Cor 1:26-31; cf. 3:21). Basically, Paul is making the same point when he asks the Corinthians, "What have you that you did not receive? If then you received it, why do you boast as if it were not a gift?" (1 Cor 4:7). That is why it makes every sense for Paul to write, "For if Abraham was justified by works, he has something to boast about, but not before God" (Rom 4:2).

Paul himself boasts quite often about what God has done in him. He has reason to boast about his ministry to the Gentiles (Rom 15:17) and about his behavior in the world, and still more toward the Corinthians, with holiness and godly sincerity, not by earthly wisdom but by the grace of God (2 Cor 1:12). Preaching the gospel is no cause of boasting for Paul, but he does boast that he has made it available free of charge (1 Cor 9:15-18; 2 Cor 11:7-11). Even if he does boast a little too much of the authority which the Lord gave him for building up and not destroying the Corinthians, he will not be put to shame (2 Cor 10:8). Paul and his companions do not boast beyond the limits God has appointed them nor in another's labor or about work done in another's field. They realize that whoever boasts, should boast of the Lord because whom he commends is the one approved (2 Cor 10:13-18). Paul does boast about the visions the Lord has given him. But about himself, he only boasts in his weaknesses, that the power of Christ may rest upon him (2 Cor 12:1-10). He boasts about the Corinthians (1 Cor 15:31), to Titus (2 Cor 7:14;8:24) and to the Macedonians (2 Cor 9:2f). Paul also feels that he and his companions give the Corinthians cause to boast of them, so that they may be able to answer those who pride themselves on a person's position and not on what is in his or her heart (2 Cor 5:12).

At times, Paul is ironical. He asks the Corinthians to accept him as a fool that he may boast a little. What he says he does not say with the Lord's authority but as a fool, in boastful confidence. Since the Corinthians are themselves wise, they gladly bear with fools. He then lists his credentials as a Jew and his numerous missionary hardships (2 Cor 11:16-19; cf. vv 20-29). Yet, he turns the tables in v 30 because he simply states, "If I must boast, I will boast of the things that show my weakness."

Paul tells the Thessalonians, Corinthians and Philippians that he will boast of them on the day of the Lord (1 Thess 2:19; 2 Cor 1:14; Phil 2:16). His comment to the Corinthians includes a mutual wish that they will likewise boast of him and his companions

There are other examples of Christian boasting. Paul advises each of the Galatians to test his or her work so that the reason to boast will be in oneself and not in the neighbor (Gal 6:4). Furthermore, Christians can boast in the midst of sufferings because they know that the suffering produces endurance, and endurance produces character, and character produces hope which does not disappoint because God's love has been poured into our hearts through the Holy Spirit (cf. Rom 5:2-5). Finally, the Philippians will have ample reason to boast in Jesus Christ because Paul will come to them again for their progress and joy in the faith (Phil 1:25f).

Thanksgiving, Blessing and Praise

Since faith is a gift and since on our own we human beings cannot do good, the basic Christian stance is that of a receiver who renders thanks for what God has done for her or him in Christ. In fact, almost every letter has a thanksgiving which Paul personalizes according to what God may have done for, in and through the given community.[42] On the other hand, the Gentiles are shown to be sinners because, although they knew God, they did not honor him as God nor give him thanks (Rom 1:21; cf. vv 18-25). The Christian stance is, "Rejoice always, pray constantly, give thanks in all circumstances; for this is the will of God in Christ Jesus" (1 Thess 5:16-18). Primarily, Christians are grateful for salvation (Rom 7:25; cf. 6:17;15:9-12; 1 Cor 15:57; 2 Cor 1:20; Gal 3:9). However, they also thank and praise one another. Not only Paul but all the churches of the Gentiles thank Prisca and Aquila because they risked their lives for him (Rom 16:3f). Paul on behalf of the collection sends along with Titus to Corinth the brother who is praised by all the churches for his preaching of the gospel (2 Cor 8:18). Moreover, such is the nature of the body that, if one member is honored, all rejoice together (1 Cor 12:26). In fact, the general attitude is that Christians are to think about anything worthy of praise and do it (Phil 4:8f).

Paul himself gives thanks. To win the Corinthians over before he addresses the difficult question of how one should dress, he commends them because they remember him in everything and maintain the traditions he passed on to them (1 Cor 11:2). But he does not commend their behavior at the Lord's Supper (1 Cor 11:17,22). Paul thanks God constantly because the Thessalonians received the word, not as the word of human beings but as it really is, the word of God at work in them (1 Thess 2:13). Later, he wonders how he and his companions will be able to thank God for all the joy the Thessalonians bring them (1 Thess 3:9). Less positive is Paul's thanks to God that he never baptized many of the Corinthians, lest someone say that he or she was baptized in his name (1 Cor 1:14-16). He also thanks God that he speaks in tongues more than any of the Corinthians, nevertheless, he prefers to speak five intelligible words that will instruct others, than ten thousands words in a tongue. Paul has periods of discourage-

[42]See 1 Thess 1:2-10; 1 Cor 1:4-9; 2 Cor 1:3-7; Gal 1:5?; Rom 1:8-15; Phil 1:3-11; Phlm 4-7. Generally, authorities hold that Paul eliminated the thanksgiving in his Letter to the Galatians because he is upset with their attitude toward the gospel and his apostleship.

ment but still thanks God who in Christ always leads him in triumph and through him and his companions spreads his fragrance everywhere (2 Cor 2:14f). Lastly, Paul does seem to like the expression, "God . . . who is blessed forever" (cf. Rom 1:25;9:5; 2 Cor 11:31).[43]

Most properly, thanks is addressed to God. Abraham did not doubt about God's promise, but grew strong in faith and gave glory to God (Rom 4:20). Christians should be fully convinced in their own minds as to what they should do about the observations of days, eating or abstaining, and then act with thanks to God (Rom 14:6; cf. 1 Cor 10:30). The Lord's Supper is a thanksgiving which Christians are to repeat. So, when Paul writes, "The cup of blessing which we bless. . . .," he is referring to our blessing of God, not of God's or Christ's of us (1 Cor 10:16;11:23-26). Whoever speaks in tongues does render thanks to God; the difficulty is that the outsider does not know what is being said and cannot say, "Amen" (1 Cor 14:16f). Paul calls on the Corinthians to help him with prayer because God delivered him from a terrible affliction in Asia (modern Turkey; probably, Ephesus). Thus, many will give thanks for the blessing granted (2 Cor 1:11; cf. vv 8-10; 1 Cor 16:8f). The proclaiming of the gospel by Paul and Timothy in Corinth extends grace to more and more people to increase thanksgiving to the glory of God (2 Cor 4:15).

The collection causes thanksgiving to God. Paul designates the Corinthians' contribution, "a blessing" (2 Cor 9:5f), and thanks God who gave Titus an earnest concern for the Corinthians and their taking part in the collection (2 Cor 8:16). Paul and those who are attending to the collection do so for the glory of the Lord and to show their good will (2 Cor 8:19). The Corinthians' generous gift will not only supply the needs of the saints but also overflow in thanksgiving to God. Hence, the Corinthians glorify God by their recognition of the gospel, and the recipients will pray for them because of their acceptance of the surpassing grace of God. Paul concludes,

---

[43]There is, of course, the discussion over the correct translation of Rom 9:5, i.e., does "God" go with "Christ" or not? Whatever the conclusion, Paul still favors the expression, "God . . . who is blessed forever" (cf. Rom 1:25).

"Thanks be to God for his inexpressible gift!" (2 Cor 9:15; cf. vv 11-14).

The churches of Christ in Judea glorify God because they hear that Paul who once persecuted them was now preaching the faith he tried to destroy (Gal 1:23f). Paul wishes that God grant the Roman Christians to think the same thing in accord with Jesus Christ in order that they might glorify God the Father. Also, for the glory of God, they are to welcome one another as Christ welcomed them (Rom 15:5-7). Paul assures the Philippians that God will supply their every need. To him be glory forever (Phil 4:19f).

Several Pauline statements about thanksgiving, of their very nature, hold for Christians of all times. The confession that Jesus Christ is Lord is for the glory of God (Phil 2:11). Although there is some dispute about exactly where Rom 16:25-27 should be located in Paul's Letter to the Romans, there is no doubt that it is a doxology to the only wise God who can strengthen the Gentiles according to the whole mystery of the gospel and to the preaching of Jesus Christ and bring about their obedience of faith. The basic point is made in 1 Cor 6:19f, "You are not your own; you were bought with a price. So glorify God in your body." The Philippians are to have no anxiety about anything; but in everything by prayer and supplication with thanksgiving let their requests be made known to God (Phil 4:6). Rom 11:36 well summarizes this section, "For from God and through God and to God are all things. To God be glory forever. Amen." Lastly, the importance of thanksgiving for Paul is noted by Peter T. O'Brien who contends that Paul mentions the subject of thanksgiving more often per page than any other Hellenistic author, pagan or Christian.[44]

---

[44]Peter T. O'Brien, "Thanksgiving within the Structure of Pauline Theology," *Pauline Studies* (Fs. F. F. Bruce; ed. D. A. Hagner & M. J. Harris; Exeter: Paternoster, 1980) 61.

8

Catalogs of Virtues and Vices[45]

The catalogs of virtues and vices come from a dualistic way of thought. Paul does tend to present reality in terms of opposites that reflect a dualistic world view, such as old age/new age, death/life, weakness/power, folly/wisdom, flesh/Spirit, already/not yet, sin/grace (righteousness), unity/diversity, darkness/light, first Adam/second Adam, works of the law/faith in Christ (cf. 2 Cor 6:14-7:1).[46]

Virtue and vice catalogs are in form and content a topos of the moral tradition. Generally, the contents are not tied to specific circumstances nor ordered according to a determined unifying or logical viewpoint. This is not to say that Paul has not added a given virtue or vice nor, perhaps, connected a given catalog to its present context. Moreover, the meaning of a virtue or vice could have been changed by Paul himself or

---

[45]This consideration will be based primarily on the presentations of Siegfried Wibbing, *Die Tugend- und Lasterkataloge im Neuen Testament, und ihre Traditionsgeschichte unter besonderer Berucksichtung der Qumran Texte* (ed. W. Eltester; BZNW 25; Berlin: Töpelmann, 1959) 77-127 and of Anton Vögtle, *Die Tugend- und Lasterkataloge im Neuen Testament: Exegetisch, religions- und formgeschichtlich untersucht* (ed. M. Meinertz; NTAbh 16 4/5; Münster: Aschendorffschen, 1936) 1,30-51,125-47,158-88. For a thorough study of the catalog form and additional information, see Ehrhard Kamlah, *Die Form der katalogischen Paränese im Neuen Testament* (ed. J. Jeremias & O. Michel; WUNT 7; Tübingen: J. C. B. Mohr, 1964) 11-38,181f,201-7,214f.

[46]William G. Thompson, *Paul and His Message for Life's Journey* (New York: Paulist, 1986) 41. See also E. Kamlah, *Die Form der katalogischen Paränese*, 28-31,201-7 and S. Wibbing, *Die Tugend- und Lasterkataloge*, 108-14.

simply by its new Christian milieu. Paul's catalogs follow
Hellenistic literature in methodology, but less so in content.
They are characteristic of the diatribe and of popular philosophy, but the intellectualism of Hellenistic ethics is absent. In
fact, the late Jewish tradition of such catalogs has exercised a
stronger influence on Paul and is, in part, the source of his
faith and theological presentation of them. His catalogs of
virtues and vices apparently originated as baptismal parenesis,
have eschatological import and relate to concrete action.

Paul in his catalogs thinks of the personal relationship of
humankind with God. The catalogs seemingly were originally
used by Christians as baptismal parenesis, and evidence of this
can still be found.[47] Paul's virtues catalogs are: 2 Cor 6:6f; Gal
5:22f; Phil 4:8. Gal 5:24, "And those who belong to Christ
Jesus have crucified the flesh with its passions and desires,"
does remind us of the baptismal passage, "We know that our
old self was crucified with him so that the sinful body might
no longer be enslaved to sin (Rom 6:6; cf. vv 1-11). Paul's vice
catalogs are 1 Cor 5:10f;6:9f; 2 Cor 12:20f; Gal 5:19-21; Rom
1:29-31; 13:13. The unit, 1 Cor 6:1-11, surely relates to baptism,
for v 11, immediately following the vice list, reads, "And such
were some of you. But you were washed, you were sanctified,
you were justified in the name of the Lord Jesus Christ and in
the Spirit of the living God." Likewise, "But put on the Lord
Jesus Christ, and make no provision for the flesh, to gratify its
desires" (Rom 13:14) reflects the baptismal formula in Gal
3:27f (cf. 5:16f,24; Eph 5:8-18).

An eschatological aspect is particularly evident in Paul's
catalogs of vices.[48] The vice catalog in 1 Cor 6:9f is twice
related to inheriting the kingdom. The point is that those who
do such things will not inherit the kingdom. This phrasing is
repeated in Gal 5:21. Moreover, the virtue and vice catalogs in
Gal 5:16-25 belong to the pericope, 5:13-6:10, where Paul
explains the right understanding of freedom, and in 6:7-9 Paul
assures the reader that God is not mocked, for whatever one

---

[47]E. Kamlah, *Die Form der katalogischen Paränese*, 3,34-8,183-9.

[48]S. Wibbing, *Die Tugend- und Lasterkataloge*, 114-7.

sows, he or she will reap. If one sows to the flesh, the harvest is corruption; if to the Spirit, the harvest is eternal life. Similarly, Rom 1:32 concludes that those who commit the vices listed are worthy of death. Finally, a number of eschatological expressions surround the vice catalog in Rom 13:13:

> Besides this you know what hour it is, how it is full time now for you to rise from sleep. For salvation is nearer to us now than when we first believed; the night is far gone, the day is at hand. Let us cast off the works of darkness and put on the armour of light ... (cf. vv 11f).

Of all the NT writers, Paul does most to connect his virtue and vice catalogs with concrete actions.[49] This is already evident from what has just been said above. However, there are further indications. The virtues list of 2 Cor 6:6f appears in the midst of Paul's description of how he and his companions have put no obstacle in anyone's way, lest fault be found with their ministry. The list of Phil 4:8 comes immediately before Paul's appeal that they do what they have heard and seen in him (cf. v 9). The pericope, Gal 5:13-6:10, not only describes the right understanding of freedom, but includes, "walk by the Spirit," "do not gratify the desires of the flesh" which prevent the Galatians from doing what they would, "led by the Spirit" and the assurance that there is no law against performing the fruits of the Spirit. The purpose of the vice catalog in 1 Cor 5:9-11 is to clarify Paul's twice noted directive, "not to associate with immoral individuals." The vice catalog in 2 Cor 12:20f lists for the Corinthians what undesirable behavior Paul fears he may find when he visits them the third time; he hopes not to have to mourn over many who sinned before and have not repented. Of the Gentiles, Paul writes that "God gave them up to a base mind and to improper conduct" as an introduction to his vice catalog (Rom 1:28; cf. vv 24,26). Finally Rom 13:13 begins with the words, "Let us conduct ourselves becomingly

---

[49]E. Kamlah, *Die Form der katalogischen Paränese*, 28-38; A. Vögtle, *Die Tugend- und Lasterkataloge* 30-5,48 and S. Wibbing, *Die Tugend- und Lasterkataloge*, 110-4,123-7.

as in the day. . . . " consequently, Paul envisions both the virtue and vice catalogs as recommending to his readers certain behavior.

Catalogs of Virtues

Now, let us briefly list the virtues and vices found in Paul's catalogs. Surely, given the above reflections, Paul approved in general the contents of these catalogs, and as we read them, we naturally react as he and his predecessors desired we should. The Greek is given only when clarity seems to demand it, and the virtues and vices are so presented that their interrelations and similarities are evident. Again, Paul's virtue catalogs are: 2 Cor 6:6f; Gal 5:22f and Phil 4:8. Attention is also called to any other use Paul makes of these virtues in his genuine letters, provided the given virtue is not treated elsewhere in this book.

1. Love (2 Cor 6:6; Gal 5:22). Lovely (*prosphilēs*: Phil 4:8).
2. Joy (Gal 5:22).
3. Peace (Gal 5:22).
4. Patience (2 Cor 6:6; Gal 5:22).
5. Kindness (2 Cor 6:6; Gal 5:22; cf. Rom 3:12). See "Goodness."
6. Goodness (Gal 5:22).
7. Faithfulness (Gal 5:22). See, "Faith."
8. Gentleness (Gal 5:23). See, "Humility"
9. Self-control (Gal 5:23; cf. 1 Cor 7:9;9:25).
10. Purity (2 Cor 6:6; Phil 4:8). See, "Holiness."
11. Knowledge (2 Cor 6:6).
12. Holy Spirit (2 Cor 6:6).
13. True (Phil 4:8; cf. 1 Cor 5:8;13:6; 2 Cor 6:8; Rom 1:18,25;2:8;9:1).
    In the word of truth (2 Cor 6:7; cf. 4:2;7:14;13:8; Gal 2:14;Rom 15:8).
14. In the power of God (2 Cor 6:7).
15. Honorable (Phil 4:8).
16. Just (Phil 4:8; cf. Rom 3:10;5:7; Phil 1:7).

17. Gracious (Phil 4:8).
18. Excellence (Phil 4:8).
19. Worthy of praise (Phil 4:8; cf. 2 Cor 8:18; Phil 1:18; Rom 13:3). See, "Thanksgiving. . . . "

The first eight virtues listed look to interaction with one's fellow human beings; the others relate more to oneself. "The Holy Spirit," "In the word of truth" and "In the power of God" reflect both God's salvation and its results in Paul's ministry, and the virtue catalog of Phil 4:8 is different from the other two. It employs terms from popular Stoic philosophy, is arranged in a definite order ("whatever is," six times; "if there is," two times) and almost all of its virtues are qualities of a good citizen.[50]

Catalogs of Vices

Paul's vice catalogs are: 1 Cor 5:10f;6:9f; 2 Cor 12:20f; Gal 5:19-21; Rom 1:29-32;13:13, and the following vices are recorded, as is Paul's use of them elsewhere in his letters.
1. Idolatry (1 Cor 5:10f;6:9; Gal 5:20; cf. 1 Cor 10:14,19; Rom 1:20-25).
2. Hating God (Rom 1:30).
3. Sorcery (Gal 5:20).
4. Wickedness, evil (*kakia* and *ponēria*: Rom 1:29; cf. 1 Thess 5:22; 1 Cor 5:8,13;14:20; Rom 12:9).
5. Wrong doing (Rom 1:29; cf. 1:18;2:8;3:15;6:13;9:14; 1 Cor 13:6).
6. Inventors of evil (Rom 1:30).
7. Meanness (Rom 1:29),
8. Inhumanity, lacking normal affection (Rom 1:31).
9. Mercilessness (Rom 1:31).
10. Arrogance (*alazōn, hyperēphania* and *physiōsis:* 2 Cor 12:20; Rom 1:30).
11. Insolence (Rom 1:30).

[50]A. Vögtle, *Die Tugend- und Lasterkataloge*, 178-88 and S. Wibbing, *Die Tugend-und Lasterkataloge*, 101-3.

12. Selfishness, selfish ambition (2 Cor 12:20; Gal 5:20; cf. Phil 1:17;2:3; Rom 2:8).
13. Foolishness (Rom 1:31).
14. Envy (Gal 5:21; Rom 1:29; cf. Gal 5:26; Phil 1:15).
15. Jealousy (2 Cor 12:20; Gal 5:20; Rom 13:13; cf. 1 Cor 3:3;13:4; Gal 4:17).
16. Deceit (Rom 1:29; cf. 1 Thess 2:3; 2 Cor 4:2;11:13; 12:16; Rom 3:13).
17. Greed (*harpax* and *pleonexia*: 1 Cor 5:10f;6:10; Rom 1:29; cf.1 Thess 2:5;4:6; 2 Cor 7:2;12:17f).
18. Speaking evil of (1 Cor 5:11;6:10; cf. 1 Thess 5:14; 1 Cor 4:12).
19. Tale bearing (2 Cor 12:20; Rom 1:29),
20. Slander (2 Cor 12:20; Rom 1:30).
21. Disobedience to parents (Rom 1:30).
22. Strife (2 Cor 12:20; Gal 5:20; Rom 1:29;13:13; cf. 1 Cor 1:11;3:3; Phil 1:15).
23. Dissension (Gal 5:20; cf Rom 16:17).
24. Division (Gal 5:20; cf. 1 Cor 6:1-8;11:19).
25. Insurrection, maltreatment by mob violence (2 Cor 12:20; cf. 1 Cor 14:33; 2 Cor 6:5).
26. Sexual immorality (*porneia*: 1 Cor 5:10f;6:9; 2 Cor 12:21; Gal 5:19; cf. 1 Thess 4:3; 1 Cor 5:1-13;6:9-18;7:2;10:8).
27. Impurity (2 Cor 12:21; Gal 5:19; cf. 1 Thess 2:3;4:7; 1 Cor 7:14; 2 Cor 6:17; Rom 1:24;6:19).
28. Fornication (1 Cor 6:9; 2 Cor 12:21; cf. 1 Cor 6:12-20;7:2).
29. Adultery (1 Cor 6:9; cf. Rom 2:22;7:3;13:9).
30. Licentiousness (2 Cor 12:21; Gal 5:19; Rom 13:13).
31. Debauchery (Rom 13:13).
32. Homosexuality (1 Cor 6:9; cf. Rom 1:24-28).
33. Stealing (1 Cor 6:10; cf. Rom 2:21;13:9).
34. Drunkenness (1 Cor 5:11;6:10; Gal 5:21; Rom 13:13; cf. 1 Thess 5:7).
35. Carousing (Gal 5:21; Rom 13:13).
36. Murder (Rom 1:29; cf. 13:9).

The first three vices look to one's relationship with God. The next twelve view the person and his or her relationship with others. Thereafter, they are all concerned with one's treatment of the neighbor. Unfortunately, Paul does not treat many of these vices in further detail.

There are two other evils or vices in Paul's genuine letters which we have not considered elsewhere. Paul speaks of "deserting God" in Gal 1:6-12 by turning to a different gospel. But there is no other gospel than the one Paul preaches. He did not receive it nor was he taught this gospel by any other human being; but through a revelation of Jesus Christ. Troublemakers in Galatia want to pervert the gospel, but anyone who preaches a gospel other than Paul's should be accursed.

Paul does not believe that homosexuality is an acceptable way of living. In the vice catalog of 1 Cor 6:9f, Paul uses two Greek words which mean male homosexuality. According to the context noted above, those who are guilty of the vices listed will not inherit the kingdom. These were things that some of the Corinthians did before they were baptized, but no longer.

Paul in Rom 1:18-31 mainly wants to establish that the Gentiles, too, are sinners and stand in need of God's salvation. In Rom 1:26-28 he writes of both male and female homosexuality. Paul contends that God has given the Gentiles up to dishonorable passions because they exchanged the truth about God for a lie and worship and serve the creature rather than the creator (v 25). Paul has joined homosexuality to an improper knowledge of God and to a resultant false vision of human living. Moreover, three times in vv 26-28, Paul writes of "natural" and "unnatural." It is "natural" for women to have sexual relations with men, and men with women. It does not seem appropriate to claim a "natural law" theory here, but Paul is telling the Roman Christians why homosexual relationships are wrong and can be used as an image to portray the condition of those who do not understand the truth about God. Finally, Paul says of male homosexuals that they are consumed with passion for one another, committing shameless actions and receiving the due penalty for their error. Consequently, although his main thought is that Gentiles are also sinners and so need salvation, Paul does view homosexuality as an evil.

To many moderns Paul's position proves disconcerting. R. Scroggs has argued that what Paul opposes is very specific forms of pederasty, namely, the adult use of male prostitutes, especially the borderline instances of effeminate free males who let themselves be used sexually. Such relationships are dehumanizing. However, according to Scroggs, Paul is not speaking to or even aware of a caring and mutual homosexual relationship between consenting adults.[51] Scroggs is aware that argument can be fairly made against his position from Rom 1, and Peter van der Osten-Sacken does just that. Since in Rom 1:26 Paul speaks of female homosexuality and does not limit himself to pederasty, Scroggs' contention is simply not correct.[52] I would add that Paul's phrasing about the male homosexuals, "consumed with passion for one another" does not seem to imply that one of them is a prostitute or someone of whom advantage is being taken. Would the moral situation as described by Scroggs have served Paul's effort to portray how false a vision of human life results from an improper knowledge of God? Whatever one's response, the relevance of Paul's teaching on homosexuality today remains a valid question. To be sure, it has to be placed in the context of the whole of Paul's teachings, especially of his directives related to the hermeneutical question and of moral theology and the insights of the modern sciences. These topics are treated to some extent below.

This chapter has studied Paul's catalogs of virtues and vices. These catalogs come from a dualistic way of thinking and are not necessarily well organized nor integrated into their present

[51]Robin Scroggs, *The New Testament and Homosexuality:Contextual Background for Contemporary Debate* (Philadelphia: Fortress, 1983) 84,101-28. Scroggs furnishes a brief summary of the debate and makes a good case for his position. E. Hamel ("Scripture, The Soul of Moral Theology?," *Readings in Moral Theology No 4: The Use of Scripture in Moral Theology* [see bibliography] 124-6) appears to agree with Scroggs's main thesis. However, he believes that Paul condemns homosexual activity in general. His conclusion is correct, but I am not sure how he reached it. His description of "against nature" as the failure to use the body in accord with God's design, is likewise loyal to Paul's text.

[52]Peter von der Osten-Sacken, "Paulinisches Evangelium und Homosexualität" *Berliner Theologisches Zeitschrift* 3 (1986) 33-5.

contexts. Certainly, Paul could have changed the meaning of a given virtue or vice. He took the catalogs over from Hellenistic literature, and even more so, from the late Jewish tradition. Paul's catalogs deal with the personal relationship of human-kind with God and others. Originally, they were apparently used as baptismal parenesis, and they have an eschatological aspect and look to concrete action. As we read the catalogs, our reaction follows Paul's lead. As shown above, the virtue catalogs look to the human person and relationships with the neighbor, but the one in Phil 4:8 is somewhat unique.

Paul has more catalogs of vices than of virtues. Some few vices bear directly on one's relationship with God, but the vast majority touch on oneself and one's interactions with the neighbor. Furthermore, anyone who turns from Paul's to another gospel is deserting God, and whoever preaches a gospel other than Paul's is accursed. Finally, Paul believes that homo-sexuality is evil, so any justification of that life style will have to be based on subsequent insights that actually demonstrate that what Paul says should be modified or is not relevant today.

Part IV

Relevance of Paul's Morality
for Christian Living Today

What relevance has Paul's teaching on Christian living or morality, today? This question becomes all the more complicated because of the present state of moral theology. At various times in the history of Christianity, different areas of knowledge undergo a crisis. Today, the crisis is in moral theology. I am not foolish enough to think that as a biblical exegete I will be able to solve that crisis. But I would like to enter into a dialogue with the reader about the value of Paul's moral teaching. At a minimum, we can hope to appreciate the complexity of the hermeneutical question: how translate what Paul says about Christian living to our present day? Let us first consider whether Paul himself suggests how we might go about answering this question and then what assistance theology might provide.

9

Paul's Directives about Our Hermeneutical Question

Paul himself helps us to determine the relevance today of his teachings about Christian living. Everything said thus far in this book would be of such assistance; this should be especially true of the overall summary below. Likewise the index will prove useful to anyone who wants to see a topic discussed in more detail. Still some aspects of Paul's thought need to be highlighted. Certainly, Paul believes that we are to do God's will and follow Christ's directives. Nonetheless, Paul himself modifies two of the latter. He acknowledges Jesus' teaching that the wife should not separate from her husband. (If she does, she is to remain single or else be reconciled to her husband.) Nor is the husband to divorce his wife. Yet, in the case of a believer married to an unbeliever who wants to separate, Paul allows separation; and as noted above, some scholars would contend that he even allows divorce. Paul's reasons are God's call to peace and the safeguard of the faith of the believing partner (cf. 1 Cor 7:10-16). Paul is also aware of Jesus' command that those who proclaim the gospel should thereby obtain their living (1 Cor 9:14). But he himself bypasses that right. The former may appear to be but a slight moderation, and the latter, Paul's personal sacrifice; nonetheless, both actions do not strictly adhere to Jesus' directives.

The Spirit, according to Paul, relates to the whole of Christian living. God's call to holiness is through the Holy Spirit (cf.

1 Thess 4:7-8). The Spirit is opposed to the flesh (e.g. Rom 8:1-4), and is the source of the fruits (Gal 5:22f) and of the gifts in the body (1 Cor 12:4-11; cf. Rom 12:4-8). The Spirit helps Christians in their weaknesses and in prayer and intercedes for us (Rom 8:26-28). Christians walk in (Gal 5:16; cf. Rom 8:4-6) and are led by the Spirit (Gal 5:18; Rom 8). There is no need to connect the Spirit with every specific moral action; rather all of Christian life and activity flows from the Spirit. This is the meaning of to be "aglow with the Spirit" (Rom 12:11).

Since God is the source of everything and so of every good deed, Christians should with prayer and thanksgiving let their requests be made known (Phil 4:6). Paul's prayer that the Philippians' love may abound more and more so that they approve of what is excellent and be pure and blameless, filled with the fruits of righteousness, on the day of Christ, is an example of Christian prayer for all times (Phil 1:9-11). Consequently, through our prayer, God may help us see the relevance of Paul's moral teaching today.

The community is the visual expression of our unity with Christ and serves as a criterion of what we should do. Our actions ought to preserve that unity by thinking the same thing and living in harmony. Unity with Christ provides us with a new self-image which naturally directs us to act in certain ways. Each of us has his or her gifts to be used for the benefit of everyone. We respect and encourage one another, share our abundance with those in need and build up the weak. The Lord's Supper expresses our unity with Christ and must be celebrated in a worthy mannner. Moreover, the community preserves moral living. Christians do not associate with immoral brothers and sisters. It may even be necessary to expel someone from the community until he or she repents of a wrong done, but the scope is always one's salvation. Once repentant, they are to be received back into the community. In addition, Christians are to respect and be subject to those who labor among them. Obviously, one's community is a significant factor in Christian living and a source for understanding and interpreting the relevance of Paul today.

Prophecy can also assist us today in determining what Paul is saying to us today. It speaks to human beings for their upbuilding, encouragement and consolation; through it others can be instructed (cf. 1 Cor 14:3-5,31). Through prophecy even an unbeliever can be called to account and so worship God and declare that God is really among the Christians (cf. vv 24f,31). Seemingly, Paul would hold that the same things are true of speaking in tongues, if interpreted (cf. v 17).

Love and Building Up

Love, too, can enlighten us about the significance of Paul's teaching on morality today. Our actions should demonstrate that love is our aim and that whatever we do, is done in love (1 Cor 14:1;16:14). We need to love the neighbor as ourselves and do him or her no wrong. The Pauline qualities of Christian love (1 Cor 13:4-8; Rom 12:9-21) allow us to evaluate our own love. Whatever Paul says in his letters which corresponds with these general principles, we should do.

One aspect of love is building up (1 Cor 8:1). Actually, like the Corinthians, we are God's building (cf. 1 Cor 3:9; cf. vv 10-17). We, too, tend to accept the saying, "everything is possible," but we need the sobering reflection that not everything builds up (1 Cor 10:23) because everything we do ought to build up (1 Cor 14:26; cf. 1 Thess 5:11; Rom 14:19;15:2). Paul's power was given to him for building up the Corinthians and not for tearing them down (2 Cor 10:8;13:10), and everything he says in the second letter is for their building up (2 Cor 12:19). Therefore, building up has to be a criterion in our judgments about the relevance of Paul's morality today.

Paul's Theme of Testing, Proving and Approval

Paul's theme of testing, proving or approval is useful in discerning the relevance of his morality for today. Paul instructs the Thessalonians, "Do not quench the Spirit, do not despise prophesying, but test everything; hold fast to what is good, abstain from every form of evil" (1 Thess 5:19-22). Certain testing is simply not genuine (Rom 1:28;2:18; 2 Cor

10:12) nor necessary (1 Cor 10:25-27). The fact is that Christian life itself can be a testing that leads to hope (Rom 5:4; cf. 14:17f). For instance, the Macedonians, in a severe test of affliction, gave generously to the collection (2 Cor 8:2). The acceptance of the man, who was expelled, back into the community and the sharing in the collection are tests of the Corinthians' obedience and love (2 Cor 2:9;8:8;9:13). Timothy and certain other Christians are said to have been tested (Phil 2:22; cf. 1 Cor 16:3; 2 Cor 8:22; Rom 16:10).

There are a number of general statements about testing which more approximate our own efforts at discernment. At the end of his Second Letter to the Corinthians (13:5-9), Paul instructs them to examine themselves to see if they are holding to their faith. They should know that Jesus Christ is in their midst, unless they fail the test. Paul himself is approved, but does not particularly want to appear to have met the test. On the contrary, he prays that the Corinthians do what is right. Thus, faith and the realization of Jesus' presence are experiences according to which we, too, can approve the good.

Paul advises that a Christian who has no reason to find fault with what he or she has decided to eat or not eat, is blessed (Rom 14:22). To the Galatians, Paul writes in a similar vein that everyone ought to test his or her own work, then the reason to boast will not be in what the neighbor has done. (Gal 6:4). Testing is twice related to the Lord's Supper. The first observation should not necessarily be limited to that liturgical event. According to Paul, factions must arise among the Corinthians that those who are genuine (approved) may be recognized (1 Cor 11:18f). Moreover, the Corinthians should examine themselves and then eat of the bread and drink of the cup (1 Cor 11:28).

The fact is that one must be spiritual to discern spiritual things; in this sense, Christians have the mind of Christ (1 Cor 2:14-16). Therefore, the Roman Christians are not to be conformed to this world, but to be renewed in mind, that they may approve what is the will of God, what is good and acceptable and perfect (Rom 12:2). Paul's prayer for the Philippians is that their love may abound more and more, with knowledge and all discernment, so that they may approve what is excellent and may be pure and blameless for the day of Christ, filled with the fruits of righteousness (Phil 1:9-11).

Of course, God's approval is the most significant. It is not the one who commends himself or herself that is accepted, but the one the Lord commends (2 Cor 10:18; cf. 1 Cor 4:3f). God approved and entrusted Paul with the gospel (1 Thess 2:4), yet Paul pommels his body and subdues it, lest after preaching to others he himself not be approved (1 Cor 9:27). For on that day the fire will test what sort of work each one has done (1 Cor 3:13).

Consequently, we are to test everything, including the relevance of Paul's morality for today. Our Christian life itself will prove the genuine nature of some of our actions. However, we must test ourselves and our actions. The Spirit and our faith and unity with Christ will help in this. Obviously, the scope of our testing is God's will, that is, to do what is right, good, acceptable, perfect and excellent. Ultimately, we seek God's approval.

The human conscience aids us in deciding the significance of Paul's teachings for modern times. For Paul, conscience looks to knowing and practical action. It can be misguided, but for the individual it possesses a supremacy and its directives are to be followed. Nonetheless, even if our own conscience would allow us to act in a given way, we are not to do so, if such action would not build up our neighbor but lead him or her into sin.

In conclusion, Paul himself assists us in appreciating the relevance of his morality today. Nonetheless, the task is not an easy one, for even he modifies two directives of Jesus. However, the Spirit, prayer and the community are always at our disposition. Prophecy can also be pertinent. Whatever we do should be done in love and to build up the neighbour. Finally we test everything and cling to the good so that with a correct conscience we act in love.

10

Theology and the Relevance of Paul's Morality

The hermeneutical task is to translate a thought from one culture and epoch to another culture and epoch. As regards Paul's letters, there are objections to such a venture. Did Paul not address his letters to specific problems that arose in a given community? Consequently, his letters are occasional and not intended as theological reflections or teachings with possible value for all times. Moreover, Paul wrote in an eschatological context. He expected that Jesus would soon come again and so, at best, he had in mind an interim morality. It was only intended to govern that brief period of time prior to Christ's second coming.

These are weighty objections. However, other evidence exists. At least one of Paul's letters is addressed to all Christians (1 Cor 1:2). Likewise, letters seem to have been read in other communities than those to whom they were addressed (cf. Col 4:16), and we do know that some of Paul's letters were collected and apparently read by various communities and individuals (2 Pt 3:15-17). Moreover, it cannot be claimed that the liturgy and practice of the Church have understood Paul's letters to be occasional and without meaning for Christians of all ages. Perhaps, most probative is the common human experience that many passages in Paul have perennial value. Witness, for example, the countless couples who want to read Paul's observations on Christian love as part of their nuptial celebration (cf. 1 Cor 13:4-10). Besides, is it not true that we are still in the interim period between Christ's death and resurrection and his second coming? Certainly the time has been extended, and today this calls for some modification of Paul's teaching. But that it should be jettisoned entirely is without justification.

How decisive, then, for any of our moral actions is what Paul writes? Probably, the most certain thing we can say about this question is that no answer is generally agreed upon.[53] Nevertheless, we can point to the elements to be considered in any attempt to answer it.

Paul's meaning in the passage must be determined as accurately as possible. Such an investigation involves a number of factors, but some of them are of particular interest. There is the *Sitz im Leben* ("Situation in Life"). In what particular situation did Paul find himself and the community addressed, when he wrote this letter? For Christian faith and revelation are always intertwined with cultural, political and social realities. The literary form that Paul uses can be even more important for our purposes. Do we have a command, a wisdom saying, a suggestion, an exhortation or Paul's personal opinion? Just precisely what do we have, and does this form or the way Paul writes tell us what he wants to say and with what authority he wants to say it?[54]

Another significant factor is that when one approaches a Pauline text, he or she has a given background, a certain academic formation and a considerable amount of human experience. No one hears Paul in an entirely passive manner. We may have considerable expertise in the area and, certainly, we have definite opinions and questions. All these and our philosophical stance or training can guide our interpretation of the text. Consequently, to get at the truth which Paul speaks

---

[53]For instance, see C. E. Curran and R. A. McCormick, "Foreward," *Readings in Moral Theology No 4*, vii-viii; J. M. Gustafson, "The Place of Scripture in Christian Ethics: A Methodology Study," *Readings in Moral Theology No 4*, 175f; cf. 151-77 and A. Verhey, "The Use of Scriptures in Ethics," *Readings in Moral Theology No 4*, 230-33; cf. 213-41.

[54]Confer J-F. Collange, *De Jésus á Paul*, 29-31; P. Sessolo, "Bleibende Bedeutung der paulinischen 'Gebote'," *Euntes Docete* 32 (1979) 191-210.

to us today, given the complex nature of the investigation, may seem like nothing short of a miracle.

Finally, our consideration of the relevance of Paul's morality today will, at least implicitly, assume faith and grace. Our hermeneutical question is, in fact, a spiritual question, for we are concerned about how we are to live our Christian lives.

Once we have determined what Paul says in a passage, P. Delhaye and H. Schürmann call for two further telling criteria to establish its authority.[55] To the extent that a moral action relates directly to the Christian response of radical love of God, it cannot be the subject of any modification. Secondly, importance should be attributed to the intensity and frequency of a moral statement in Paul. In addition, J. M. Gustafson queries whether we are bound to use a "method of ethics," should such be found in Scripture.[56] To an extent, the answer to this last question has to be "yes"; for instance, how reasonable would it be to ask about the relevance of Paul's thought for today and not to follow what he writes that bears on this hermeneutical question?

As Paul himself asserts, the Christian community plays an important part in our moral lives. After all, the community did establish which books were sacred and has always claimed the presence of the Spirit and its own right to interpret what the NT writers are saying. To be sure, we Christians fight over how the community does this, which community is the "true" one and what authority it has in our individual lives. On the other hand, Paul is confident of his own authority and maintains that the other apostles and his fellow workers likewise exercise authority. For him a community preserves moral living. Consequently, moral decisions which go against those of one's community should, at least initially, be suspect.

At times, there is an evolution in our understanding of a moral action. S. Zedda notes this of some OT teachings

---

[55]P. Delhaye and H. Schürmann, "The Actual Impact of the Moral Norms of the New Testament: Report from the International Theological Commission," *Readings in Moral Theology No* 4, 88, cf. 78-104. S. Zedda (*Relativo e assoluto*) has dedicated his whole book to the modern relevance of Paul's moral thought.

[56]J. M. Gustafson, "The Place of Scripture in Christian Ethics," 175f.

(divorce, polygamy and the law of retaliation) modified in the NT.[57] Above, we observed that Paul does expand and somewhat modify Jesus' teachings on marriage and on living by the gospel. Certainly, the possibility of a more profound and thorough understanding of our moral activity exists. However, it is not always easy to identify this and its consequent influence on what we are to do.

The search for accurate knowledge is a constant in our lives. Human experience and the scientific accomplishment of modern times are of no small assistance in this search. For example, psychology can alert us to the degree of a person's freedom and the complexity of one's motivation; on the other hand, sociology helps us to discover whether something is a social phenomenon limited to a given epoch, such as the place of women in society. But the wisdom of Paul's instruction to test everything remains. If specialists in a given area of study are not able to agree in their analyses of a problem or situation, which opinions can we use in coming to a personal decision? Moreover, are we dealing with a different human being than Paul was? Is it not basically the same human person whose make-up we now know much better?

Surely a present moral situation may well differ from what Paul is saying. However, difference alone does not mean that what Paul writes has no relevance. As far as possible, the degree of the difference has to be determined, for an action may well be somewhat different and be considerably less culpable than Paul thought, but even today, it remains an evil action.

Furthermore, we need to be alert to two tendencies. Unless I am wide of the mark, there is today a tendency to trivialize human actions. People live as if it does not really matter what they do. Whether this attitude is caused by the conviction that only God brings salvation, by a deep, not well detected pessimism about human dignity and significance or whatever, I am not sure. I feel much surer of the reality. Also, we naturally

---

[57]S. Zedda, *Relativo e assoluto*, 29f.

tend to rationalize whenever a given moral directive hits too close to home.

Perhaps, the best starting point in our effort to judge the value of what Paul says to each of us individually about our Christian life is to assume that what he writes is true. Such is the traditional approach, and this assumption automatically challenges everyone to articulate why Paul's teaching does not bear on the decision to be made. This direct dialogue with Paul, with attention to his overall moral teaching, has greater likelihood of being objective.

General Conclusion

Through compositional criticism, this study considered the letters of Paul commonly accepted as genuine. Paul addressed his letters to Christians, not to all humankind, and our investigation limited itself to what Paul writes about morality or Christian living. Part I reviewed the sources of morality. God is the source of every good action, and with his grace we act morally. Normally, for Paul, God acts *through* Christ. However, Christ with his grace and power also can bring about our Christian living, as can the Spirit. The Holy Spirit is opposed to the "flesh," and is the source of the fruits and gifts in the body. Christians walk and are led by the Spirit who brings discernment and holiness. Of course, our prayer recognizes God as the source of moral living and solicits his activity in our lives.

Likewise, human morality is founded on what God did in Christ. Salvation, which Paul expresses in numerous ways, supports Christian living. However, his main way of speaking of salvation is our unity with Christ. Despite our differences, we are to live in peace and harmony. Our unity with Christ gives us a new self-image and makes us a new creation. Consequently, we do not act as before. Particularly, we die with Christ to sin, the flesh and passions, to live a new life. We shun the worship of idols.

Our lives ought to manifest our righteousness and to be worthy of the gospel, for we act from faith. Grace and the promises of God lead to moral activity. We are now free to serve God and righteousness, to love and serve one another and to be holy. Wisdom, knowledge and thinking are gifts of

the Spirit and principles of human action. Of course, they are
to be subordinated to love. Furthermore, Paul's teachings on
resurrection, the Parousia and judgment furnish moral directives. We live in the hope of things unseen. When the Lord
comes, we do not want to be found unprepared, but awake
and blameless in holiness. We build with care. God is not
mocked. What one sows, one reaps.

The Christian community is to preserve morality. Christians
do well not to associate with immoral or troublesome
members. It may be necessary to expel someone for his or her
own good, but if they repent, they are with love to be taken
back into the community. Christians should try to think the
same thing in the Lord and live in fellowship. Visits and
hospitality are aspects of Christian life, for they demonstrate
love, support and encouragement of one another. The "strong"
should bear with the "weak" and esteem them. All should act
in good conscience and do everything to build up one another.

Part II demonstrated that Paul gives any number of moral
directives to communities or individuals. "Encourage" is used
often by him, and all of his letters have an "imperative" section.
Christians should do the good, and certain actions are designated as "good". Furthermore, Christians walk by faith and in
the Spirit; they walk in newness of life and in the light, avoiding
all fleshly desires.

To evaluate fairly Paul's social teachings one has to view
them in connection with his very strong emphasis on union
with Christ, the expectation of Jesus' imminent return and the
desire not to put anything in the way of the ministry. Paul
calls for harmony in the community. Although he himself is
not comfortable with discussing how men and women should
dress, he apparently saw the situation in Corinth as an obstacle
to the ministry. Nor should Christians bring a charge against a
brother or a sister before a pagan judge. Rather they ought to
solve these disputes themselves. They are to support one
another and respect those in authority.

For Paul, husbands and wives are equal partners in marriage. Paul passes on Jesus' teaching about divorce, but slightly
modifies it. The peaceful living of one's faith allows the believing partner to let an unwilling unbeliever separate. If they

stay together, the believer sanctifies the spouse and the children. Paul is aware of different callings, but given the situation, he holds that celibacy is better than marriage because the former state is free of worldly anxieties and permits one to concentrate on the Lord and how to please him. Paul is not in favor of marriage to unbelievers.

The Lord's Supper is to be celebrated in his memory and in a worthy fashion. One cannot partake of it and of pagan banquets. Even the collection for the poor in Jerusalem is God's grace and doing. A free and generous gift to it manifests love and promotes Christian unity. The Corinthians are to be like Christ who became poor so that others might be rich. Moreover, the Lord loves a cheerful giver. Finally, Christians face death with hope, good courage and abounding in the work of the Lord. They die and rise with Christ, ultimately victorious.

Paul directs us to imitate himself and Christ. We are to center our lives on Christ and his resurrection; in him we are free and not slaves. Still we join in Christ's suffering. In imitation of Paul's ministry, we proclaim the gospel and seek not our own advantage but to please everyone. We dedicate ourselves to the good of the community, handle personal accusations adroitly, find Christ's power in our weaknesses and use an experience like imprisonment as an opportunity for deeper union with Christ, concern for others and the spread of the good news.

Part III studied the human person, gifts and how to await the Parousia. Paul's concept of the human person is Jewish, and the whole person can be considered under different aspects, e.g., spirit, heart, soul, body and flesh. "Spirit" and "flesh" are the most important. "Spirit" designates human openness to the Spirit; flesh, human beings in so far as they are inclined away from God and to sin. Moreover, each of us has a conscience through which we reflect on the truth and move to decision and action. One's conscience can be misguided, but he or she is not, therefore, to be looked down on, but built up because Christians act out of love.

In fact, love is at the center of Christian morality. Love is our aim and how we are to do everything. It is a still more excellent way and what we owe everyone. "You shall love your neighbor as yourself" fulfills the whole law. However, in 1 Cor 13:4-8 and Rom 12:9-21, Paul further delineates the qualities of love. Christian freedom is intended for loving service, and our love can increase. Love is found in the lives of Paul and his communities.

Our faith, our total trust in God (thus, Paul does not speak often of our love of God), is pure gift. We act out of faith which works through love. Christians live by faith and stand firm in it, and preaching the gospel message and the use of gifts accord with one's faith. Of course, hope is connected with one's faith. We hope in Christ, the resurrection and in being sons and daughters of God; however, we cannot hope in what is seen. Hope characterizes all of Christian life. Through it we boast of hard times and develop patience, endurance and character. We do not grieve, but make bold proclamation.

An aspect of our unity with Christ is peace which results from having our minds set on the Spirit and from following the norm of the new creation. The kingdom of God is joy and peace. Despite hardships, Christians rejoice always; they rejoice in hope, in the right and in one another. It is well known that joy is a major theme in Paul's Letter to the Philippians. Comfort accompanies peace and joy. For instance, the resolution of his dispute with the Corinthians comforts Paul.

Christians are to be holy. Paul is holy in his ministry and recommends holiness to his communities. Holiness can bear on one's attitude toward sexuality; for example, the celibate is anxious about how to be holy in body and spirit.

Service and ministry are part of Christian living while "slavery" is a more intense statement of service. There are many kinds of service, but each is to be done in love. Christ ministered and even became a slave. Ministers are to be faithful and act with integrity. We should put no obstacle in the way of our ministry; rather like Paul, we should be willing to become everything to everyone. Labor and work are other expressions for ministry. Paul mentions his labors and work in his communities and speaks of his fellow workers. Physical work, too, becomes Christians, and ultimately, those who do good are rewarded.

Paul feels obliged to preach the gospel among the Gentiles. His reward is to do it free of charge. He does it with conviction and loyalty, despite suffering and a lack of eloquence. Yet he shares not only the gospel, but his very self. The Philippians and Timothy join him in this preaching. Proclamation, and even "speaking," can mean to preach the gospel. Paul and his companions are not peddlers of God's word, but by the Spirit, they preach not themselves but Jesus Christ. Teaching, too, is a gift to be used to build up one's fellow members. Those who preach and teach should be able to live from this service.

Prophecy and speaking in tongues are also gifts. Unless what is said in tongues is interpreted, prophecy is the better gift because it builds up and encourages others. Both gifts should be so used that order prevails at liturgical gatherings.

We are to be humble and meek and to work out our salvation in fear and trembling. Christ himself gave us an example of humility. Like Paul, we hold in earthen vessels the treasure of the gospel. Also, we should be willing to live in harmony, to associate with the meek and not to be conceited. There is no reason to be puffed up. Rather we should share Christ's meekness and let our gentleness be known to all. Our patience and endurance build character. If we boast correctly, it is in God who achieves everything in us. Most impressive is Paul's boasting in his weaknesses because in them the power of Christ rests on him. Likewise, we can boast in our own weaknesses and in our suffering because God's love is poured into our hearts.

Since we are receivers of God's gift of salvation, the basic Christian act is to thank God in all circumstances. Likewise, we are thankful for one another and what we do for each other. The Lord's Supper is our major prayer of thanksgiving. In general, we glorify God for what he has done, is doing and will do for ourselves and others.

Paul does have catalogs of virtues and vices. These come from a dualistic way of thought and from Hellenistic literature and the late Jewish tradition. Paul's catalogs deal with the personal relationship of humankind with God and with oneself and others. Originally, the catalogs were apparently baptismal parenesis, and they have an eschatological aspect and look to

concrete action. Even today, our reaction to reading the catalogs follows Paul's lead. There are more catalogs of vices
than virtues, and the catalog in Phil 4:8 is somewhat unique.
Finally, to turn from Paul's to another's gospel is to desert
God, and Paul does hold homosexuality to be an evil. Any
justification of homosexual relationships will have to depend
on subsequent human insights.

Doubtless, all of us would be happier, if the hermeneutical
question about the relevance of Paul's theology today were
not so complex. This is all the truer because moral theology is
presently undergoing its own crisis. Paul himself does point us
in the right direction. To be sure, the whole of his morality
bears on the question. But certain aspects of his thought are
more pertinent. However, we should be cautious, for Paul
himself feels free to modify Jesus' teaching on divorce and, to
be sure at a different level, on living from the preaching of the
gospel. Nonetheless, for Paul all of Christian life flows from
the Spirit, and our prayer to God can lead us to approve the
good. The community preserves moral living. Prophecy and
speaking in tongues, too, can guide us. Love is our aim, and
Paul leaves us in no doubt about its true qualities. We should
serve and love the neighbor as ourselves, and everything we do
should build up other Christians. We are to test everything.
Our Christian life itself provides some testing, and the scope of
all testing is to discover God's will and what is acceptable.
Finally, a correct conscience, based on Paul's gospel, can guide
us.

The occasional and eschatological nature of Paul's letters
does not limit their message to the past. The letters were read
in other communities and collected together at an early date.
Much of their content is of perennial value, and we still live in
that interim period before the second coming. What we need is
the right hermeneutic, not total rejection of Paul's thought.

Paul's meaning in a given passage has to be determined as
accurately as possible. So, we consider any evidence that bears
on his meaning and remind ourselves that we ourselves approach a text with definite biases. The closer Paul's teaching is
to the Christian response of radical love of God and the more
its intensity and frequency, the less it is to be modified. Even

our methodology should be influenced. The Christian community plays an important part in our correct interpretation of Paul's teachings. Moreover, we can gain a more profound and thorough understanding of given moral questions from human experience and the modern sciences. Of course, such insights put some of Paul's statements in perspective.

As Paul advises, we should test everything. Differences do not automatically mean that what Paul says is without import today. Since there does seem to be a modern tendency to trivialize human activity and none of us is above rationalizing, perhaps, it is best from the start to assume that Paul is right; at least, we will be challenged to clarify why not.

For Further Reading

Robert J. Daly *et alii, Christian Biblical Ethics, From Biblical Revelation to Contemporary Praxis: Method and Content* (New York: Paulist, 1984) 23-177, 211-301. The authors help us to see how difficult it is to determine a methodology or hermeneutic. Pp. 61f,97-103,114-138 and 289-295 are of particular interest. The book is intellectually stimulating; well worth reading. However, as the authors themselves admit, the majority of people will not be able to follow their methodology in reaching moral decisions. Also, I have reservations about some of James A. Fischer's interpretations of Paul.

T. J. Deidun, *New Covenant Morality in Paul* (AB 89; Rome: Biblical Institute, 1981). Good. Alerts us to the Old Testament and covenantal background of some of Paul's moral terminology and to law as a necessary corollary to Christian love. However, Deidun limits himself to only certain texts and emphasizes the covenant more than Paul himself does. Nor is it clear that he appreciates the hermeneutical problem.

Joseph A. Fitzmyer, *Paul and His Theology: A Brief Sketch* 2nd. Ed. (Englewood Cliffs, NJ: Prentice Hall, 1989). An excellent synthetic presentation of Paul and his theology in their broad outlines. Pp. 97-107 provide a perceptive discussion of Paul's ethics. Very good bibliographical data.

Victor Paul Furnish, *Theology and Ethics in Paul* (Nashville: Abingdon, 1968). Still a valuable book. In general, Furnish provides a very good overall view of Paul's thought. However, Furnish overemphasizes the eschatological in Paul (e.g. p. 215) and does not see the Spirit as a guide for the believer in practical matters of conduct. Furnish's understanding of "mystical union" is unusual (p. 176). Finally, if the law is from God, how can Furnish claim that Paul holds that it "prods sin into activity" (p. 143), and what is one's view of human nature, if a Christian cannot be said to be "an achiever or performer," granted that God's power is the source of every good action (pp. 200, 205)? Furnish has an excellent survey of the nineteenth and twentieth centuries' interpretations of Paul's ethics and offers an extensive bibliography.

Victor Paul Furnish, *The Moral Teaching of Paul: Selected Issues* 2nd Ed. Rev. (Nashville, Abingdon, 1985). This second and revised edition is a definite improvement over the first. However, Furnish's hermeneutic is not sufficiently developed to give a correct hearing to what Paul's morality may say to us today.

Roger Mohrlang, *Matthew and Paul: A Comparison of Ethical Perspectives* (Cambridge, University Press, 1984). Considers five topics of major importance to the motivation of ethics in their writings: law, reward and punishment, relationship to Christ and the role of grace, love and inner forces. The sections on Paul are well done. But he overstates Paul's position on the Spirit and on grace in his morality and misunderstands the context of 2 Cor 5:10. Excellent bibliography.

Jerome Murphy-O'Connor, *Becoming Human Together: The Pastoral Anthropology of St. Paul* 2nd. Ed. (Good News Studies 2; Wilmington, Delaware: Michael Glazier, 1982). A perceptive book which views community as the key element of Paul's thought. Murphy-O'Connor's understanding of Paul's anthropology and christology is, however, less convincing.

"The Actual Impact of Moral Norms of the New Testament: Report from the International Theological Commission." Text by Hans Schürmann, Introduction and Commentary by Philippe Delhaye *Readings in Moral Theology No. 4: The Use of Scripture in Moral Theology* ed. Charles E. Curran & Richard A. McCormick (New York: Paulist, 1984) 78-104. The majority of the other articles are also relevant to our topic and are of a superior quality. However, I do have serious reservations with J. Sanders' article; less so with S. Hauerwas'. E. Schüssler Fiorenza's is fine, but the thought on pp. 374-8 needs further development and to be placed in a community context. C. E. Curran (pp. 189f) holds a non-traditional position on divorce; otherwise, his article is also of high quality.

William C. Spohn, *What Are They Saying about Scripture and Ethics* (New York: Paulist, 1984). Spohn considers the six different ways in which theologians are using Scripture to determine moral guidance. He does not limit himself to Paul's epistles and grants that the practical level of morality is given the least attention by the authors surveyed. Well worth reading in an attempt to see how moral theologians have employed the New Testament in their thinking.

William G. Thompson, *Paul and His Message for Life's Journey* (New York: Paulist, 1986). This very practical and useful book belongs to the area of adult education. Thompson dialogues with Paul about his life, dying and rising with Christ, God's plan, individuals and communities and prayer. The consideration on pp. 130-6 looks more to a Protestant audience.

Thomas H. Tobin, *The Spirituality of Paul* (Message of Biblical Spirituality 12; Wilmington, Delaware: Michael Glazier, 1987). Generally, this is a perceptive book. I would disagree with some of his interpretations of Acts, and I wonder if his stress on "power" in Paul does not downplay the personal and if Tobin's understanding of "universality" is correct.

Subject Index

Do not associate with bad companions, 53
Do what makes for peace, 49
Excommunication, 122
Firm in the faith, 53, 89
General attitude of, 107
Guileless as to what is evil, 45
Hope in God and in Christ, 91
Hope in the resurrection, 91
Hospitality, 59
Joy in one another, 91
Labor is not in vain, 53, 66, 74
Live by faith, 89, 127
Live in fellowship, 132
Live in harmony, 49, 102
Live in hope, 74, 104
Living sacrifices, 53
Lowly bodies to be glorious, 69
Not tempted beyond strength, 64, 104
Not to please themselves, 50
Observance of civil laws, 61
Prayer, 107, 122
Rejoice always, 91, 107, 134
Respect for another's conscience, 68
Seek the good of our neighbor, 49, 54, 96
Servants of the gospel, 74
Should associate with the humble, 102
Should build one another up, 49, 55, 68
Should know God's will, 53
Should never be conceited, 102
Should share, 59, 60, 132
Spiritual worship, 53
Stand firm in the Lord, 69, 74
Steadfast, 53, 66
Testing, 124
Thanksgiving, 106-09, 122, 135
Their prize, an imperishable crown, 53, 74
Think the same thing, 132
Through love to be servants, 86
Try to please everyone, 55, 74
Unity with Christ, 28, 29
Wait in patience, 90
Walk by faith, 132
Walk in newness of life, 132
Walk in the light, 132
Walk in the Spirit, 74, 132

Were to eat together, 59
Wise as to what is good, 45
Church (local), 12
Churches of Christ
Glorify God, 109
Circumcision, 30, 31, 33, 59
Civil leaders, 55
No need to fear, 61
Ministers of God, 95
Power from God, 61
Will praise and protect, 61
Clement
Worked with Paul, 97
Clothing, 74, 132
Veil on women's heads, 59
Collection, 25, 34, 47, 92, 107
"A blessing", 108
"Good", 55
"The Grace of God", 36, 65, 108
Causes thanksgiving, 97, 108, 109
Christian unity, 29, 65, 74, 133
For poor in Jerusalem, 26, 59, 60, 65, 133
Manifests love, 133
Mutual sharing, 74
Paul eager to do, 65
Service, 35
Colossians, 31
Comfort, 18, 19, 91, 104, 134
Amidst afflictions and sufferings, 93
Relates to peace and joy, 92
Theme in Corinthians, 93
Communities
Characterized by love, 86, 87
Directives to, 51
Mutual support, 74
Community
"Excommunication", 44, 54
"True"?, 128
Authority?, 128
Established sacred books, 128
Harmony in, 40, 50, 74, 132
Interpreting Paul's teaching, 137
Interprets NT writers, 128
Local or universal, 44
Look to the interest of others, 50
Must be disposed to forgive, 45
Presence of the Spirit, 128
Preserves moral living, 44, 122, 128, 132, 136

Index of
Scripture References